THE FAMILY CLINIC

A Book of Questions and Answers

JOHN L. THOMAS, S.J.

is the author of: THE AMERICAN CATHOLIC FAMILY
BEGINNING YOUR MARRIAGE
THE CATHOLIC FAMILY
MARRIAGE AND RHYTHM
CATHOLIC VIEWPOINT ON MARRIAGE AND FAMILY

and co-author of: MARRIAGE AND THE FAMILY
A GUIDE TO CATHOLIC MARRIAGE
SOCIAL ORIENTATIONS

The
Family Clinic

a book of Questions and Answers

by JOHN L. THOMAS, S.J.
Member of the Institute of Social Order and
the Department of Sociology, St. Louis University

THE NEWMAN PRESS · WESTMINSTER, MARYLAND
1958

Imprimi potest: Leo J. Burns, S.J.
Provincial, Wisconsin Province
June 20, 1958

Nihil obstat: Edward A. Cerny, S.S., D.D.
Censor Librorum

Imprimatur: Francis P. Keough, D.D.
Archbishop of Baltimore

September 29, 1958

Contents

v

THE FAMILY CLINIC
A Book of Questions and Answers

There Are No Simple Answers to Questions on "Steady Dating"

We're deeply concerned over what we hear about the evil of steady dating. We have two children in high school now. Sue is a freshman and Jim is a junior. Both have plenty of dates, it seems, and we haven't paid much attention to them since we know the boys and girls they are with and keep careful check on when they must come home. Are we being careful enough? What do people mean by "steady dating" at this early age?

⌘⌘⌘⌘⌘⌘⌘

MANY serious parents are asking these questions, and I may as well tell you at once that there are no simple answers. The best I can do is to lay down some basic principles and spell out a few definitions. You will have to make the applications in the case of Jim and Sue.

First and foremost, you do have a serious obligation to supervise the friendships of your children. Although you rightly desire them to develop social skills and confidence in dealing with others, you must guide and protect them during this process, for they lack experience and mature judgment.

Only silly, irresponsible parents insist that their children are mature enough to manage such relationships without guidance.

1

Second, in our society, association between boys and girls is started at a relatively early age. Some parents like to pretend that their children are sexless. Fortunately, or otherwise, nature ignores such pretensions.

Your children do have sex, and it is important to recognize that because we tolerate such early association between the sexes, the sexual drive is called to their attention about the same time that they start the practice of dating.

Since the personal expression of this drive is still a new experience, they do not yet appreciate its strength, nor have they acquired the inner controls needed for its regulation.

Third, it follows that this is an important period for instruction and guidance. On the one hand, young people are striving to assert their independence; on the other, they are meeting new problems with which they need help.

If you have been careful to give them the necessary instructions concerning the nature and purpose of sex, you will now have their confidence when they meet new experiences. Briefly, they must be given some understanding of how sexual stimulation and arousal occur in themselves and in others. Thus they will learn to control their own feelings and to avoid causing difficulties for others.

Nothing is to be gained by being shy in this matter. Young people must understand that certain acts (of affection) are, or may become, sexually stimulating, and they must face this fact honestly.

Finally, the term "steady dating" has many meanings. Among couples old enough to marry, it generally implies legitimate exclusiveness of friendship leading to possible engagement and marriage.

Among young people who can have no thought of immediate marriage, it apparently includes a variety of patterns, extending from the convenient agreement that a given pair can safely rely on each other for dates, to the exclusive, affectionate, and intimate association of a couple which differs in no way from steady dating among marriageable couples.

Clearly, this latter form is morally dangerous and unreasonable since there can be no immediate prospect of marriage.

As parents, you must carefully distinguish among these different forms of steady dating. Make every effort to retain the confidence of your children and be frank in pointing out to them why you are opposed to all forms of steady dating which represent more than a convenient agreement to go places together over a limited period.

Explain to them that you trust them but not human nature. If they are normal boys and girls, they cannot engage in intimate displays of affection without moral danger. If they deny this, they are either fooling themselves, or they are underdeveloped.

Finally, you will be wise to cooperate with other like-minded parents in supplying some means of recreation and entertainment for your maturing children. This is your surest way of knowing where and with whom they are.

Young people must have something to do. You can throw them back on their own limited resources, or you can help them find entertainment which you can approve.

How to Deal with a
Husband Who Never
Takes His Wife Out

What do you think of a man who never wants to take his wife out? We've been married five years now, have three wonderful children, and I guess we'd be considered a happy married couple. Ed is a good provider. I know he works hard, but when he comes home, he just wants to eat and sit around reading the paper or watching television. He says he's tired. So am I, but I feel it will do us both good to get out once in a while. How do I get him out of this domestic rut we've fallen into?

≈≈≈≈≈≈

PEOPLE are the queerest monkeys, Mary! Some wives complain that their husbands are never home, and some complain that they're home too much. It's possible that the reason is pretty much the same in both cases.

The problem stems both from thoughtlessness and the different ways that men and women may define the meaning of marriage. Perhaps it will help you meet this problem if we consider its sources.

First, there is thoughtlessness. Married people tend to take each other for granted. Particularly once the children start coming, husbands and wives slip into fairly clearly defined roles more or less automatically.

Somebody has to pay the bills, and father goes at his job with drive and energy. Somebody has to take care of the house, the meals, the laundry, the shopping and the children, and mother applies her energy to this never-finished daily routine.

It is just at this point that a couple can fall into a fatal domestic rut that eventually puts them far apart in a vocation which was designed to bring them ever closer together.

If a couple forgets that marriage is a life-companionship which grows by doing things together, he may lose himself in his job, and she may lose herself in her housekeeping or children. Whether you are fully aware of it or not, Mary, you have sensed this possibility.

Marriage is a twosome. It starts that way, and once the turbulent years of childbearing and child rearing are passed, it continues that way. You must grow together all through marriage. This means you must enjoy playing together as well as working together.

Unfortunately, some people don't think of marriage in that way. For them, life is divided into a man's world and a woman's world. Once they are married, women are supposed to retire into their world of the home, and men are to be occupied with theirs.

This definition of marriage leaves little room for together-ness and companionship as husband and wife. Briefly, it says: This is a man's world, and women will be happiest if they learn to accept it.

Now, Mary, I don't know whether your husband is just thoughtless or whether he holds a different view of marriage than you. If the latter, there probably isn't much you can do to change him, since he may be following the pattern of his father before him and feels that this is the way it should be.

However, you might point out that his father more than likely devoted more time than he to his wife and children, since he couldn't escape to the passivity of watching television.

Chances are, your husband is merely thoughtless. Let him see that you really appreciate his hard work in behalf of the family, but show him that you both need to get out together as a couple.

Husbands sometimes forget that men have gained a 40-hour week, but mothers with children must still work seven days out of seven. It may help toward this realization if you let him take care of the children for a good stretch on Saturday or Sunday while you are away.

Most men aren't experts at empathy—the ability to put themselves in their wife's shoes and to realize her special feelings and problems. A taste of baby-sitting may help.

Keep working on him, Mary. Prudent couples make it a point to go out together at least once a week. They feel this draws them closer together and gives them a better view of their marriage. I might add that it also keeps them from forming the habit of seeking all their entertainment separately.

Marriage is for life. The companionship of courtship should blossom into the intimate togetherness of parenthood and old age, not into the mere usefulness of partnership in a business.

Are You Too Young
to Marry? It Depends
Upon Your Maturity

When is a girl old enough to marry? Bill and I are very much in love. We've been going steady for the past few years and want to get married when I finish high school. I'll be 18 then and Bill will be 22. He's in his second year of college and can go to work with his Dad any time he's ready. Father doesn't say much, but Mother insists I'm too young. Do you think we should wait until I get more schooling?

~~~~~~~

WELL, Jane, there's no simple answer to your question. In spite of what some people say, the best age for marriage cannot be stated in terms of years. It must be figured out in terms of maturity. Perhaps we can help you solve your problem by pointing out a few facts about marriage and maturity. These are points you need to consider in making a sensible decision.

First, what is marriage? It is a life partnership or companionship formed by a man and woman who love each other. As a couple, they want to share life together. They feel they need each other, are good for one another, and can be happy together throughout life.

But marriage is a very special type of partnership. Love

9

between husband and wife is creative and productive for they love each other, body and soul, as man and woman. In other words, marriage means babies.

It means family life, with children to care for, to love, to raise, and to train. In marriage, you dedicate yourself to the service of life with the man that you love.

Second, what kind of maturity is needed for a happy marriage? There are several types of maturity: physical, psychological, social. Let's see what they imply. Physical or biological maturity means that you have grown up sexually, that you are capable of fulfilling your role in reproduction.

Strictly speaking, girls are capable of having babies at a fairly early age—around 14 or 15, but they are sexually mature only around 18 or 19 when they are fully developed and can assume the responsibilities of childbearing and child rearing without strain.

Psychological maturity means that you have learned to stand on your own feet and can face problems when they arise. This maturity is not directly related to age, but some experience of life is needed to acquire it.

It implies a sense of responsibility, reasonable control over your feelings and emotions, ability to love and cooperate with others, and willingness to face difficulties squarely.

If you are over-dependent on others, if you dodge difficult tasks and responsibilities, if you constantly blame others for your mistakes and failures, if you are not sensitive to the feelings and rights of others, you are psychologically immature.

Social maturity means that you are capable of assuming the obligations of marriage in American society. This implies that you are able to be a real companion to your husband, can run a home, and can take care of children under the social conditions in which your marriage will place you.

These social conditions are important. When you marry, you accept the economic and social position of your husband. The family unit you form with him must manage on the money he earns, and its social position will depend largely on the type of job he holds.

Hence social maturity implies different qualities for different marriages. For example, if you marry someone in the professions, you must have sufficient education and training to be his companion and to move in his social circle.

If your husband's work will require him to move frequently, you must be prepared to adjust to new situations and to make new friends. If his income will be small, you must be able to adapt to the living conditions he can afford.

You're right, Jane, I'm not going to tell you what to do. Think it over. I have given you the principles for a solution. You're in love, but love is not enough. How mature are you? Since your husband is getting a college education, don't you think you'll make him a better companion and wife if you get some further schooling too?

Do You Think
In-Laws Are Trying to
Control Your Marriage?

We have been married three years. There's one child, aged two, and my wife is pregnant again. Our marriage has been very happy, but there's one fly in the ointment —the in-laws. We make a practice of going to her parents for dinner on the first Sunday of every month, and it's really getting me down! I haven't anything against them. They're nice people, I guess, only I feel they're trying to control our marriage. My wife says I'm inconsiderate. This is becoming a problem because I honestly think she is too attached to her parents. Am I thinking straight on this point?

∾∾∾∾∾∾

YOU may be right, Bill, and then again you may not be. There are many angles to this so-called in-law problem. It may help to consider some of them before attempting to figure out a solution for your case.

In the first place, in-laws are not out-laws. Your wife— and you—were cared for, protected, instructed, and loved by parents for many long years before your marriage.

The bonds of affection, respect, and love between parents and children are second in strength and endurance only to

13

the bonds uniting husband and wife. The parent-child relationship is a long time in developing. It does not cease to exist by the fact of marriage.

Second, because every child represents the living expression of their own marital love, it is normal for parents to have their child's interests at heart even after marriage.

They wish their child to be happy, and because they have some experience of married life, they may find it difficult not to give advice or to offer assistance.

Third, families differ greatly in the closeness of parents and grown children. Some families are close-knit unions, binding sisters and brothers, parents and children firmly together with bonds of affection, mutual service, and companionship. Other families maintain rather loose family bonds.

When husband and wife come from different family backgrounds, each may find it difficult to appreciate the other's attitude toward relatives and interprets it as either over-attachment or lack of considerateness.

Finally, marriage necessarily involves a weaning process in which one's primary family loyalty is shifted from the parental circle to the new unit under formation. Just as in infancy, this weaning process requires adjustment by both parent and child.

Parents must understand that their child now has a new center of interest around which love and loyalty must be primarily focused. The child must also recognize that marriage requires this shift of love and loyalty from parents to partner.

In a sense, this shift constitutes the final step in growing up and the first step in building marital unity. Married couples should expect their partners to retain their love and affection for their parents. Indeed, as two-in-one-flesh, they should expect to share in this as much as possible.

They must also be tolerant of differences in demonstrating this love and affection in different family circles. On the other hand, each has the right to expect the partner's primary love, affection, interest, and loyalty to be centered on his own marriage.

As I see it, Bill, your problem stems from a little lack of understanding on the part of both of you, and probably on the part of your in-laws, plus a rather foolish mistake made at the beginning of your marriage.

There is no good reason why you should have dinner with her parents on the first Sunday of every month—or with your own parents, for that matter! This is a confining, senseless arrangement which you will do well to modify.

There are several ways of doing this without needless offense or hurt feelings. You can break the pattern by planning a trip on that Sunday, by getting yourselves invited out by some of your friends, or by having them over for some special reason. Once the pattern is broken, it should be easy to work out some more agreeable way of visiting your in-laws. At any rate, you and your wife must recognize that in-laws can be shown the affection and love they deserve without your being chained to them.

My Husband Could Earn More if He Just Had More Drive

I know money isn't everything, but you can't do much without it. We managed all right when we first married. I was working and we had less expense. Now, with four children to take care of, the bills just keep piling up. My husband doesn't have enough drive. I feel he could get a better job if he tried. He claims he's doing his best. What can I do?

≈≈≈≈≈≈

WELL, you can go on nagging him until you drive him to drink or to another woman. The technique is simple. It is being applied effectively every day in our society. Start out by showing him how miserable you are. Make him feel inferior and incompetent by telling him what other women's husbands are doing. Insinuate that you could do a better job than he if you were the breadwinner. It's bound to work! Soon he'll start spending less time at home. He may even start drinking a little. Go after him for that! It won't be long before you'll have less money and he may not come home for a day or two at a time. Then you can put your children in a home or leave them with mother and get your old job back. And one more marriage goes on the rocks!

No, you don't want that solution. Are there others? Let's analyze your situation. First, when you married, you accepted your husband for better or worse. This really means that you loved and accepted him as he was. Maybe you didn't think about it at the time, but this implied that you agreed to establish a family and live according to the standard of income he would be able to supply. At marriage, then, you could make a reasonable estimate of what your financial position would be. The earning capacity of the average male in our society depends primarily on his education, his previous work experience, his native talents, and his drive. These were fairly evident at marriage and you accepted them.

Second, marriage is a partnership in parenthood. As you stated correctly, money isn't everything, but the family enterprise must be based on a solid economic foundation. Now, if you look around, you will notice that some families manage to stay out of debt and some are always floundering in a sea of bills. Why does this happen? It's not just a matter of income size. Two factors are generally operative here. First, some families are in debt because they foolishly attempt to live beyond their obvious means. Second, some couples don't know how to manage their income. They always have too much month left over at the end of their money.

What can you do? First, ask yourself if you are foolishly trying to live beyond your means—beyond the standard you implicitly accepted at marriage? Second, are you using your income to the best advantage? Do you keep a budget so that you can tell your money where to go, or do you spend it as the occasion arises and then wonder where it went? Make a list of your income and your expenses. At the top of your expense account place those items which are absolutely necessary for the family's existence. These must be paid first. If you have any money left over, you may use it for other items, but they come second. Then, take an account of how you run your household. Do you buy everything in the way of prepared food and clothing, or are you making a real contribution as housewife?

Finally, perhaps your husband isn't doing his utmost. Nagging won't help. Get him to work together with you in drawing up the budget. Make up your minds that you can and will balance the books. On the day of marriage you lovingly took each other for what you are. You still have each other, plus the grace of vocation. Surely you have what you need for happiness and success.

Is It All Right for
a Boy to Marry
While Still in School?

Do you think it's all right to marry before your husband has finished school? I'm 20 and Ed is 24. We've been going together for several years and are really very much in love. But Ed needs two more years of college before he finishes his professional preparation. Our parents want us to wait. We'd like to marry now. Is it foolish for us to marry while Ed is still in school?

≈≈≈≈≈≈≈

IT would be nice if there were a clear-cut answer to your question. Unfortunately, several distinct factors are involved, and you will have to weigh them separately if you wish to make a prudent decision. Many young couples are facing this same problem because our dating and courtship practices make it possible for them to fall in love before they are ready to assume the full responsibilities of marriage. At the same time, as our civilization becomes more complex, more years of formal education are required before young men are prepared to support a family.

Let us review some of the pertinent factors. First, what is marriage? Marriage is a loving companionship and life partnership in the family enterprise of bearing and rearing children. It implies that you are willing and reasonably prepared to fulfill this function. Marital love is normally creative and productive, seeking its mature expression in a child. Although a small percentage of couples may be sterile, the vast majority of American husbands and wives are fertile. Hence, marriage means parenthood.

Second, a young husband trying to finish his education is scarcely in a good position to start a family. Modern education is expensive in itself, and few students are capable of holding an outside job while applying themselves seriously to their studies. Unless they obtain financial aid from their parents or some other source, they will find it difficult to continue at school and support a family. Many parents are willing to send their children through school; most are reluctant to support their children's families in addition.

Some young couples may enter marriage with the intention that the wife will work until the husband has finished his education. This solution has several highly questionable aspects. Either the couple are gambling on the possibility that the wife will not become pregnant, or they are planning to use rhythm in order to avoid a pregnancy. The first alternative is quite unrealistic, judging from available statistics. The second must be viewed with considerable caution. Not only is it extremely difficult for young couples to practice rhythm morally, but the tension and frustration associated with the practice render early marital adjustment hazardous. Finally, when the wife sacrifices herself to send her husband through school, marital relationships may assume a parent-child character, with the result that the husband may tend to look for another partner once he leaves school to take his place in the world.

Third, but you insist you are very much in love. Although the intensity of your love may not in itself be a sufficient guarantee of success in marriage, given the freedom tolerated in modern courtship, it does make the preservation of chastity very difficult. You must face your situation realistically. If past experience leads you to conclude that you will not be able to observe premarital chastity, you had best marry and work out a solution on that basis.

On the other hand, there is no good reason why a sincere young couple, even though very much in love, cannot preserve chastity. Happiness—and sanctity—imply that both inside and outside of marriage you learn self-control. Of course, you must make full use of grace and common sense. Through prayer and the sacraments you will obtain the strength and motivation to love each other as Christians, while common sense will teach you to avoid those displays of affection which may arouse unwanted excitation.

You and Ed have a real problem. In reaching your decision take all the factors into account. Remember, you are choosing a life vocation, not a year or two of companionship.

Should We Move
for a Better Job
in Another City?

We've been married nearly ten years, have five wonderful children and a home of our own. Jerry and I had to make some real sacrifices in the beginning. They didn't matter because we knew what we wanted. Now, just as we are settling down to enjoy things, he's offered a big job in another city. He wants to take it, but I tell him we have everything we need to be happy here— friends, a home, and sufficient income. Don't you think I'm right?

∞∞∞∞∞∞

IT does seem you are doing very well where you are, Madge. Most couples married only ten years would envy your position. You've made some early sacrifices and they have paid off well. You've become attached to your home and your circle of friends. Jerry is doing all right financially now. Why give all this up and move to a strange city just for the sake of a promotion? Money isn't everything, especially when you have enough to live on comfortably.

This is sound reasoning on your part. No doubt, Jerry has given some thought to these things too, yet he still wants to move. Is he being selfish, thinking only of himself? Does he have a false sense of values? Does he have the right to

25

forget about the sacrifices you have made and move his family wherever he pleases? Let's try to look at the situation from his point of view. It's not likely that he has suddenly grown selfish and unconcerned about those whom he loves.

In America a man with ambition and drive picks out a career in which there are reasonable opportunities for advancement and promotion. He hopes that if he works hard and uses his talents well, he will get ahead. He knows that he must compete with others at every step, for other men are also trying to advance. Hence, every promotion means more than an increase in pay. It is a public acknowledgment of his effort and ability. He feels he is achieving some of his goals, he is being given a chance to use his talents to the fullest.

Because he is the breadwinner of the family, he sees no necessary conflict between his desire to advance at work and his role in the family. Provided he is careful to be a good husband and father in the family circle, he feels that his promotions reflect to the credit of the family. As he sees it, he is working so hard only for them, in the first place. Of course he is proud of his accomplishments and enjoys the added prestige which goes with each advance, yet these would have little meaning in the long run if his family were not happy.

That's about the way your husband sees it. Do you still think he's being selfish in wanting to move? The effort and ability which have paid off so well up to the present are now being rewarded and offered a wider field of operation. Can you blame him for feeling he should take the new position?

Chances are you can persuade him to remain where he is. To be sure, as head of the family, he has the right to make the decisions about moving, but most American husbands soon learn that authority which is not accepted willingly is dearly paid for in the long run. Yes, you can probably talk him out of it. Whether he admits it or not, he will feel penalized and cheated. Think it over. It is your discomfort at moving against the frustration of his career. Who's being selfish?

How Early Should
Parents Start Religious
Training of Children?

We have one child eighteen months old and another on the way. Both my husband and I have resolved that our children will get a sound religious training because we realize how important this is for their happiness. Our problem now is where to begin. When should one start the religious training of children?

≈≈≈≈≈≈≈

A FEW years ago in a talk to Catholic mothers, Pius XII answered your question directly. "It is your task from the cradle to begin their education in soul as well as in body; for if you do not educate them they will begin, for good or ill, to educate themselves." And a little later in the same talk he said, "Love the catechism and teach your children to love it; it is the great handbook of the love and fear of God, of Christian wisdom and of eternal life."

The Pope's words are clear enough. Together with modern sociologists, child psychologists, and our own common sense, he tells us that the child starts learning from birth, and that this learning process is both rapid and lasting. What does the child learn? That depends upon the family circle which affects him. For the child, the family circle

29

represents the world. In a very real sense he is the "product" of his family. What he learns comes from them.

When should he be told about God, the Blessed Mother, the angels and the saints? We only have to formulate this question to realize how foolish it is. There is no one time when the child should be told these things. Since he starts learning in the cradle, he must be subjected to an environment, an atmosphere, in which God, the Virgin Mother, the angels and the saints are realities.

When should he be taught religion? The truths of religion must first be lived in the home by you, his parents. Your attitudes, actions, and expressions convey to the child through every avenue of knowledge by which he is capable of learning, the great religious realities. When should he be taught to pray? Obviously, simple prayers can be taught as soon as he can learn other things.

But isn't the pre-school child too young to learn about God? Only one who doesn't know children could ask that question! After all, what does it mean to "know about God"? What does the average adult know about God? Essentially, it is that God is our loving Father, that He created us out of love and destined us for happiness with Him throughout eternity, that consequently we should reverence, love, and serve Him if we are to develop, to really "grow up." The child readily grasps the truth that God is lovable and to be obeyed. The reality of the angels and saints presents no problem to the child—provided he sees that these realities are accepted in his family circle.

As the Pope reminds us, you have already started training your child because he has already started to learn. On the sensory level, he is capable of noticing the sound of the voice, the look, the gesture, the caress, the act of rejection or punishment. On the emotional level, he can sense the feelings of those around him. He reacts to love, fear, joy, hate, and tension. As he develops, he will learn to speak and understand language. Then he will receive ideas, sentiments, evaluations, and judgments. All through these stages he is steadily learning. What he learns about religion will depend on you.

Christian parenthood is a noble vocation. By patiently molding into His Image the human clay which the Divine Artist has confided to your loving care, you are sharing in the work of God. You are just starting your work. It will be finished only when your children stand beside you as mature, full-fledged "citizens of two worlds."

My Wife Thinks
I Don't Pay Enough
Attention to Her

My wife seems to think I don't pay enough attention to her. Maybe I am a little forgetful at times. I work hard all day and have a lot of things on my mind. She knows I love her and the children. Why else does a man knock himself out earning a living? We've been married for 6 years now and I figure she ought to know by this time that I think she's tops. Are all wives this way?

∞∞∞∞∞∞

MANY husbands ask the same question, and the stock answer they receive is always in the affirmative. Women, we are told, need attention and affection. Wise husbands should play up to this feminine weakness. This answer makes men feel strong and magnanimous, and it puts women neatly in their place. I have some serious doubts about the validity of this interpretation. If we stop to analyze the situation, we discover that most wives are merely asking for a fifty-fifty break.

In the average well-run family, who gets the lion's share of attention? If it is not the baby, it is father. When he comes home over-tired, everybody soon learns about it. Is he having trouble at work? He expects his wife to listen to his gripes. Does he have to make a trip? His bag will be efficiently packed with fresh linens and all that he is likely to need. Does he stay home sick? Then even the baby ceases to become the center of solicitude and attention. This is all perhaps as it should be. He is the breadwinner, the head of the family, and much depends upon him. But the point is, he does receive a great deal of attention and he assumes that he has a right to it.

Now marriage is a companionship, a partnership in a very exacting enterprise. Woman's role as wife and mother in this enterprise necessarily confines her to the home. Her contribution to the well-being of the family equals that of her husband. Her domain, her job, is the home. It is here that she makes her contribution. Just as her husband feels needed and important because he earns the family support, so she feels needed and important in managing the home. Is she queer, or does she display feminine weakness because she would like to have her role acknowledged as she does her husband's? How many husbands like to be taken for granted?

Furthermore, unlike her husband, her role confines her largely to the home and to the company of immature children so that she has limited opportunities for adult companionship. Is it strange that she should seek this companionship from him? A cynic has remarked that women like a strong, silent man because they think he's listening, but most wives who have spent all day with the children are hungry for a little adult conversation.

If you think it over honestly, you will probably have to admit that your wife's complaint about lack of attention is merely her way of asking for an even break in the partnership. You take her solicitude and attention for granted as a kind of natural masculine right. Is she wrong in asking for a return in kind? Ask yourself, what things do you do together? When were you last out as a couple? When did you last notice how she was dressed, her cooking, the way she manages the home and trains the children?

Remember, marriage is a partnership for life in which you both find fulfilment of your basic needs and aspirations. God willing, you will be companions for a long time to come. Are you growing together in mutual understanding and intimacy, or are you merely cohabiting? Not a few husbands and wives have made this latter mistake. They reach the golden years of the empty nest, when their children have left home, feeling more like co-workers in a completed enterprise than companions in the venture of life.

How Can You Tell
if a Boy Will Be a
Good Marriage Partner?

Everyone keeps telling us how important a good marriage partner is, but how can you recognize one before marriage? Like most other girls, I want a happy marriage. I'd like to have children, a home, and a loving husband. What should one look for in a future mate? I've dated quite a few boys and like most of them. How can I tell which one would make a good husband?

❦❦❦❦❦

YOUR short question calls for a long answer, Mabel. I suppose every thoughtful girl reaching maturity has this question more or less in mind. Because marriage will be so important for your happiness and sanctification, your first step is to pray earnestly and steadily that God will help you find a good partner. Once you decide that marriage is your vocation in life, this intention should be included in all of your prayers.

How can you recognize a good future mate? Of course, it must be someone that you can respect and love. Unfortunately, love is not enough. You can love someone—or think that you love him—even though there is little or no chance that you could build a successful marriage with him. Marriage means partnership in parenthood. It implies being able to live with a person as well as being able to love him. Because premarital love necessarily centers on mere companionship, it cannot be the sole criterion for selecting a marriage partner.

But love, or perhaps more correctly, emotional involvement, is such an exhilarating experience that few couples pay much attention to other criteria once they have reached this stage. Further, since frequent association between marriageable men and women normally leads to love, it is important to keep these other criteria in mind when selecting your dating companions. What should you look for?

First, you should have similar views in regard to religion. There are many types of "Catholics." Some are Catholic in name only; some are superficial, practicing more or less out of habit; and some are serious and sincere. Because the overall purpose of the marriage vocation is mutual sanctification, you should select a partner who will truly assist and support you in serving God.

Second, you should choose a partner who is willing and able to support a family. There's no great mystery here! Marriage means partnership in parenthood. Just as you must be ready to fulfill your roles as wife and mother in the home, your husband must be prepared to support a household. This implies that he has some training or skill, a sense of responsibility, and the ability to hold a steady job. If a man has made no effort to prepare himself for an adequate job, if he displays little sense of responsibility either in his attitude toward work or the use of his money, he's a poor marriage bet. You're not likely to reform him after marriage, and remember, your position in society will depend almost entirely upon his ability to support you and the children.

Third, your partner should have a balanced personality.

Can he control his temper? Does he treat others justly and with respect? Does he "go to pieces" under strain? Does he have any insight into his own character or does he always blame others for his failures and lack of success? Is he stubborn and self-centered in dealing with others and with you? If some of these traits upset you before marriage, reflect that you will experience them much more intimately and personally in marriage. They are signs warning you of his true character.

Finally, don't marry a man with the hope of reforming him. I suppose every woman is a born mother, endowed with perennial desire to sympathize, console and remodel. However, if a man is old enough to marry and still needs to be reformed, don't flatter yourself that you are the divinely appointed agent to do so. If his own mother, his friends, the school, and society couldn't achieve this, you had best leave him up to God. Marriage wasn't meant to be a reform school.

My Wife Wears
Herself Out in Dozens
of Church Affairs

My wife wears herself out in church affairs. She manages to get involved in just about everything. If there's a drive, she's sure to head it. If it's serving hot lunches to the kids, she'll be there. Are we going to have a bazaar? She'll head one of the committees. I tell her other women can do something for a change. Why must the same few do all the work?

❧❧❧❧❧❧

WELL, Bill, have you ever attended a regular meeting of the Knights of Columbus, the Eagles, the local labor union, or of any other voluntary organization? If you have, I think you know the answer. Studies show that only around five per cent of the members attend the business meetings regularly and consequently do most of the work. The other members are what we call "pork-barrelers" in the labor movement. They come in for the gain, the entertainment, or because it's the thing to do, but they make little contribution in terms of personal effort and sacrifice.

It tends to be the same story in church affairs. In almost every parish one finds a little nucleus of faithful workers ready to volunteer whenever any work comes up. The remainder are like the guests invited to the wedding feast in

Our Lord's parable—they all have good excuses for not coming. Of course, some really have, and I suppose all think that they do. Come to think of it though, it's strange that the same people always have a "good" excuse, while others who are just as busy somehow always seem to find time to cooperate. It is interesting to note that this pattern first shows up while these people are still in school. The students who are "pork-barrelers" grow up true to form. Maybe they just had a head start on others in learning to make good excuses.

So you see, Bill, there's nothing unusual about what's happening in your parish. Of course, it's not fair and just. When there's work to be done in the parish, everybody should be willing to make a sacrifice of time and energy to see it through successfully. This is as clear an obligation as supporting the parish financially and follows the same basic criterion: each according to his ability. The point is, how do we make people generous? How do we get them to give up their sloth and that calculating attitude which prompts them to give only when they clearly foresee a personal return? Since preaching hasn't accomplished it, perhaps good example will. However, as you may observe, it hasn't been very contagious up to the present, either.

In regard to your wife, then, you have only one question to ask. Does her outside activity keep her from doing a good job as wife and mother at home? There are a few mistakenly pious souls who get themselves so involved in outside activities that they don't find time to fulfill their primary obligations in the home. This is apparently not your problem. Rather, you feel that your wife is being imposed upon.

Perhaps I have been a little hard on the "pork-barrelers." Some of them may feel timid and insecure, fearing to put themselves forward. Some may be new arrivals, waiting to be asked. At the same time, the workers are not without their immediate rewards. Generally, they are the type that really enjoy doing things for others. They appear happiest when they are busiest. At any rate, Bill, thank God you have married a generous wife.

How Can Parents Best
Give Their Children
Sex Instruction?

All this talk about the need to give sex instruction in the home has some of us parents worried. We know there's a need and we recognize it's our job, but we're not very sure about how we should tackle it. Our oldest boy is in high school, and one of our daughters is finishing eighth grade. How can we best help them?

❧❧❧❧❧❧❧

I SUPPOSE there are few questions which cause serious parents more concern than the one you have asked. There are many reasons. Each child develops somewhat differently. Modern society places great emphasis on every phase of sex. Americans no longer agree on the meaning of sex so that acceptable conduct in this area is neither clearly defined nor uniformly practiced. Because this problem is so complex, perhaps the best way to answer your question is to set down a few observations and principles for your guidance.

First, what should be your aim? Since sex, in its real meaning, is the special human quality of manliness or womanliness, your goal is to train your boys to be mature Christian men, and your girls to be mature Christian women. This means that sex education must never be separated from general education. Boys and girls grow up to be men and women precisely as male and female persons. Part of this growing up process necessarily involves the knowledge and control of their reproductive powers. Hence as male and female persons, growing boys and girls must gradually acquire some understanding of the "facts of life" plus all those religious, moral, psychological, and emotional attitudes toward these facts which adult Christians should have. Your aim as parents is not to preserve ignorance (lack of knowledge) in your children, but innocence (lack of personal experience).

Second, it follows that there is no special time which can be set apart for training in chastity, modesty, sex hygiene, or sex information. Individual children differ, and growing up is a gradual process. Hence training should be gradual, adapted to the needs of each individual child, repeated and reviewed like all teaching, and aimed at anticipating the needs of the growing child.

Third, it is obvious that you can give this training adequately only if you have the confidence of your child. For this reason it is important that both father and mother start the religious and moral instruction and guidance of the child from the cradle. Thus you will be identified as teachers in the child's mind, and he will acquire the habit of turning to you when problems arise. Some parents foolishly hand over this early instruction and guidance almost entirely to the school, with the result that the child's spiritual life is closed to them by the time he reaches puberty.

Fourth, you cannot give what you do not have. Unless your own views in regard to sex are balanced and thoroughly Christian, you cannot train your child properly. This should be obvious, but some parents have never developed mature attitudes toward sex in their own lives, so they communicate their fears, anxieties, and misconceptions to their children.

Fifth, you must be realists. Your own experience has taught you a great deal about normal sexual development during puberty and adolescence. You have considerable knowledge of the conditions and circumstances within which your child is growing up. Call on your common sense and the grace of your vocation to instruct, guide, and direct him until he reaches maturity. Act on the assumption that your child is normal, with normal curiosity, drives, desires, and reactions under temptation. Some parents evidently don't like to face the fact that their children are probably normal. They like to regard them as sexless creatures, alien to normal desires and reactions.

These observations are general and were not meant to meet all of your problems. If you would like an excellent treatment of the subject, read Father Henry Sattler's little book, *Parents, Children, and the Facts of Life* (St. Anthony Guild Press, Paterson, N. J. It also appears in a popular, paper-back edition). You have an important job, but if you use common sense and the grace of your vocation, you have no cause for anxiety.

How Can Husbands and Wives Work for Each Other's Sanctification?

We were told at marriage that religion was one of the most important forces binding us together in life. Our pastor spoke very beautifully about the obligation of husbands and wives to work for each other's sanctification. Since we've been married, however, we're not so sure what all this really means. How can we bring religion more fully into our marriage?

✻✻✻✻✻✻✻

YOUR concern about religion in marriage is shared by many other serious couples. Trained as religious individualists from their youth, they find it difficult to share their spiritual world with others. Even in marriage, their religion remains a strictly personal affair, yet they feel it should have some additional meaning for them as a couple. If it is a bond of unity, it should be experienced as such. If they are to sanctify each other, they would like to know how to go about it.

Perhaps I can clarify your problem by pointing out a few necessary distinctions. There are two principal ways in which religion functions as a visible bond of unity in married life. First, it supplies a common set of practices and devotions. Second, it offers a common or shared interpretation of life.

49

In regard to the first, husbands and wives can attend church and the sacraments together, they can pray together, and they can cooperate in various activites related to the Church. Even apart from the added graces they receive from their efforts, their common participation in these practices binds them more closely together. It is a basic law of human relations that people who cooperate in doing things together are inevitably drawn together by their shared activity.

Second, a common interpretation of life clearly serves as a bond of unity. When couples share the same moral system, cherish the same goals in life, define suffering, sacrifice, and self-denial in the same Christian terms, their life together develops within a unifying framework of values. They see life's joys, sorrows, and routines alike because they start from a common point of view.

But marriage is also a school of perfection. How do husband and wife sanctify each other? In addition to serving as ministers of grace to each other through the sacrament which unites them, they work for their mutual perfection in the two ways listed above. This is to say, by encouraging and supporting each other in the performance of religious practices, they more easily fulfill their obligations in the service of God. Even more important is their mutual service in developing a Christian interpretation of life. Engrossed in the busy struggle to make a living and raise a family, one or the other may lose sight of their real purpose in life or ignore important Christian values. The partner is there to recall these truths through words and example. As new situations arise, the couple help each other develop a Christian point of view. Likewise, there is encouragement to growth in spiritual understanding. By sharing what they read, and hear, and think, both can deepen their spiritual lives.

So you see, religion is pretty much what you make it in marriage. It will serve as a bond of unity and an instrument of mutual sanctification to the extent that you approach it as a couple. Pray together, of course, but above all, learn to think and speak together as Christians.

Mixed Marriages

SIR,—I, too, contracted a "mixed marriage" and throughout the first 10 years clung precariously to my faith.

Because my husband had deeply religious but Protestant convictions, there was often a lack of "sweet accord and geniality" in the home.

By the grace of God he was received into the Church shortly before our son was born (I confess my own example contributed little to this) and "the sweet accord" came just before his sudden death when he remarked: "I wish I had your faith" (trust in God). And I replied: "And I wish that I had your goodness."

In conclusion I would say that any Catholic contracting a "mixed marriage" must not only *practise* his religion, but know *why* he does . Prayer will accomplish the rest.

He must also be prepared to feel at times a great spiritual loneness, for however much in love may be, fulfilment of that love incomplete when beliefs are divided.

2. Herold   T.O.S.F.
Surrey.

What Are the
Right Answers About
Necking and Petting?

What's the morality of necking and petting on a date?
Everybody seems to have a different opinion. Whenever
we discuss it, all the fellows insist that they have re-
ceived conflicting answers from various spiritual directors.
How can I know what's right?

≈≈≈≈≈≈

AS YOU have probably learned, Bill, some of the confusion concerning the morality of necking and petting
stems from the different ways these terms are defined.
Spiritual directors agree on the moral principles involved;
their answers will differ according to the different meanings
which are attributed to the terms *necking* and *petting*. The
best way to clarify your problem is to by-pass these ill-defined
terms and apply our moral principles to real practices, whatever they may be currently called.

First, let us be clear concerning the general moral principles involved. In using our sexual faculties, as in all our
conscious activities, we must follow the order of right reason.
Reason tells us that since sex deals with the co-principles of
life, and since only God has dominion over life and the co-
principles of life, we must use sex according to the divine
plan. This plan specifies that sex is to be used and enjoyed

only by those who are joined together in the marriage bond. All other deliberate use of sex is contrary to right reason and seriously sinful.

Second, although all normal men and women have sexual faculties which fulfill an important function in the development and maintenance of their entire system, these faculties must be stimulated or aroused if they are to perform their special reproductive function. The phenomenon of sexual excitation is highly complex, differing considerably in men and women and also among individuals of the same sex. Imagination, affection, intent, and physical contact play important though variable roles in stimulation. However, there are actions which are designed by their very nature and regardless of the intent of the agent to cause sexual stimulation. These intimate physical contacts are generally summarized under the term *petting*. Their use outside of marriage always involves a violation of right order and is consequently sinful.

Further, some routine displays of affection such as kissing and embracing may become highly stimulating to one or both parties either because they are prolonged, or because of the manner in which they are performed. In this situation they become the source of serious temptation and must be avoided. Some young people do not like to admit that they become sexually aroused under these circumstances, but if they are honest with themselves, they will have to acknowledge that something more than routine affection colors their activity.

Third, the practice of dating in our society serves two functions. First, young people enjoy doing things together as couples. Second, through this association they acquire some knowledge of the opposite sex and eventually select a marriage mate in the courtship process. Neither casual dating, steady dating, nor the final stages of courtship confer any sexual privileges. Although courtship, as the immediate stage before marriage, may involve considerable display of mutual affection, at no time may one indulge in actions which are by nature designed to be directly sexually stimulating. Neither may one intend such stimulation or take pleasure in it should it occur.

Well, Bill, you may feel that I have taken the long way around in answering your question. It is the only practical way. You must know the moral principles involved, you must have some understanding of how sex is aroused in yourself and in others, and you must be sincere in facing your problem. The mature man regulates his actions according to right reason. Such conduct demands self-control, but then, you really haven't grown up until you have acquired this.

We Are Expecting
Another Baby and
My Wife Is Unhappy

My wife is giving me a rough time. I'm in the dog-house now because she has just learned that she is pregnant again. We have two children already and she decided that's all there were to be, at least for a while. Of course her present condition is all my fault! She's going to be hard to live with for the next few months. What can a Catholic husband do? I'm willing and able to support a family, but I'm getting tired of having her pose as a victim. Doesn't she have some obligations, too?

❧❧❧❧❧❧

THE family situation which you describe, Harry, is apparently becoming quite common in what is loosely called the American middle class. More precisely, it characterizes those who aspire to or who have moved into this class. It is not easy to deal with because it stems from a complex set of attitudes and misunderstandings prevalent in contemporary society. It will clarify our thinking if we analyze these in some detail.

First, there is confusion about the meaning of marriage. Marriage has come to be looked upon primarily as a companionship. This is the way it is defined in the majority of textbooks, in popular writing, and in the public mind. But marriage is more than a mere companionship. It is by its very nature companionship with a purpose. This purpose is parenthood. Parenthood is not something incidental to marriage, a mere matter of choice. It is inherent in the very nature of marital companionship, for love between man and woman tends to be productive and creative. Its true significance, its ability to provide for the couple's fullest development and self-realization lies in its reproductive character. The companionship of husband and wife grows and finds real fulfillment only in the childbearing and child rearing process.

Second, there is confusion about the role of woman in marriage. Women have moved rapidly toward greater social equality and freedom in the modern world. In itself this change is all to the good. However, in gaining their freedom, some women have lost their direction. They're not sure where they're supposed to be going. They've grown confused about where their true self-fulfillment and consequently happiness is to be found. In particular, some forget that marriage is a partnership in which both spouses must contribute their share according to the different roles which each can fulfill. The marriage contract includes a life-long meal ticket for the wife only if she assumes her marital duties. Some wives apparently believe that their right to be supported involves little or no obligation on their part.

Third, there is confusion concerning sexual differences in men and women. It appears that some wives, either because of false attitudes, previous training, or because they find other emotional outlets, experience little difficulty in by-passing normal marital relations. Hence, if they are opposed to having more children and are Catholic, they expect their husbands to abstain from relations too. If husbands refuse, or find this difficult, they accuse them of selfishness, or of being inconsiderate, or even of being over-sexed.

What is the answer? Well, some wives lose their husbands before they learn it. Some don't lose their husbands, but sacrifice the profound happiness which true companionship and partnership in marriage offer them. Some do grow up with the passing of time. Have patience, then, Harry. At marriage you agreed to help your wife reach happiness in this world and the next. If you can gradually lead her to a deeper understanding of the meaning of life and of marriage, you will have carried out that agreement in the best possible way.

What's the Best
Way to Promote
Vocations for Children?

My wife would give just about anything if one of our boys would turn out to be a priest. I fully share her attitude in this regard but feel we must be very careful in the way we go about encouraging a vocation among our boys. I feel that she tends to offer a little too much encouragement at times. What's the best way to promote vocations among your children?

～～～～～

B EFORE answering your question, it may be helpful to consider what we mean by a vocation to the priesthood. Clearly, it is a calling from God to serve a special function in His Church. This does not mean that God normally makes a special revelation to the individual that he has been called. How, then, does one recognize a vocation? In answering this question, theologians usually distinguish between what they call the subjective and the objective aspects of a vocation. The subjective aspect consists not so much in sentiments or feelings but in the right intention of the aspirant, joined to the necessary physical, intellectual, and moral endowments. Hence anyone who aspires to the priesthood with the unique motive of consecrating himself to the service of God and the salvation of souls, and at the same time possesses, or is willing to acquire, the necessary virtues and learning, shows that he is called by God to the priesthood. This subjective calling is completed and made formal by the objective calling of the appropriate ecclesiastical authority who accepts the candidate for ordination.

It follows that you are primarily interested in promoting the subjective calling, that is, the desire to consecrate one-self to the service of God and the salvation of souls. How can you encourage and promote this desire among your children? First, perhaps the most important thing from the natural point of view will be the respect and esteem which you yourselves show toward the priesthood and priests. Children are quick to sense their parents' attitudes. In choosing their life work, these attitudes necessarily play an important role.

Second, stimulate interest through conversation and reading in the great heroes of the faith, the saints and religious leaders who fought so nobly for Christ. Young people like a challenge. They are easily inspired by an ideal which demands the best that they have. Perhaps it may start out as mere wishful thinking, but they all dream about doing great things some day. Why not give direction to this thinking by showing what others have done?

Third, teach them about the work Christ came to do. Help them to see that His work is not finished, that He has put it into our hands, and that we have the privilege of cooperating with Him in saving the world. I would stress this point. Too often religion is presented as little more than a set of rules and a more or less selfish sharing in prayer and the sacraments. Hence, youth views it more as a restraint than a challenge. Teach your children to see the work of the Church as an extension in time and space of the work of Christ. He wants us to help Him. What will we do for Him?

Fourth, you are correct in feeling that care should be used in the manner in which vocations are promoted. Hold up the right motives, and stress generosity, love of work and study, and manliness. Some parents confuse lack of initiative, childish emotionalism, and easy conformity with true piety. A vocation must be built on more sterling qualities.

Finally, you should pray earnestly to the Lord of the Harvest. "The fields are white with the harvest, but the laborers are few." If you ask humbly and sincerely, can He refuse your repeated request?

I'm Getting Tired of
Trying to Please My
Over-Critical Husband

My husband doesn't like a thing I do around the house. We've been married for almost six months and things aren't getting any better. I've learned one thing, though, his mother is just about the best cook, housekeeper, buyer, and so on, since Eve set up shop. I'm getting tired of trying to please him. Nothing I do seems to be just right. How does one handle such men?

※※※※※※

SOME young males are strange animals, Martha. They gripe while they're home with mother, and they gripe when they're in a home of their own. It may be that they have been spoiled as children, but I rather feel it is their thoughtless way of asserting and getting attention. They want to be noticed, to feel important. Like all youthful striving for independence, their thinking is self-centered and critical of others. What others do for them is taken for granted as if they deserved it. This is a youthful stage. Unfortunately, some men and women never develop beyond it.

Is this the type you married? Let's not pass hasty judgment. There may be other factors involved in the situation which merit further consideration. In the first place, the early months of marriage call for numerous adjustments and changes. Domestication is a gradual process, and while they're getting used to it, some young men feel they are giving up more of their freedom than they bargained for. At times, young brides are more possessive and domineering than they realize. The inexperienced groom may react by asserting his independence in curious ways. One of these may be dissatisfaction with the way you run the house.

Second, is it possible that you are over-sensitive about your performance around the home? Are you trying too hard to be a success? Sometimes when we are starting out at a new job, our anxiety causes us to see criticism where none was intended. If we are trying very hard to please, even the failure to notice our efforts may be interpreted as an implicit condemnation of what we've done.

Third, many young husbands are not aware of their brides' normal feeling of insecurity in their new roles. They may carelessly throw out references to their mothers' way of doing things without stopping to think that their brides may take this as a reflection on their own efforts. The young bride tends to be so sensitive because, to some extent, she feels she is in competition with her husband's mother. She wants to prove that she is just as competent and efficient as her older rival, forgetting that she has already won the battle by getting some mother's son to marry her.

If a little analysis reveals that your present troubles represent nothing more than the normal "growing pains" of early marriage, you have little to fret about. Both of you will become more sure of yourselves as time goes on. When your husband thoughtlessly brags about his mother, reflect that some day you hope to have boys who will grow up to brag about you. You'll like that, won't you?

On the other hand, if you've married an habitual griper, you have a different case on your hands. Marriage calls for adjustment and adaptation, but these should be mutual. It is not wise to make all the concessions in any partnership. If your husband expects you to do so, it will be prudent to set him straight from the start. Quarreling won't help matters under these circumstances. State your position once and then ignore his later comments. You have no reason to feel insecure. After all, you can always burn his toast, and you can always say "no," can't you?

Why Does the Church
Harp on the Evils of
Mixed Marriage?

Why is the Church always harping on the evils of mixed marriage? I know of several right in our neighborhood which are very successful. Besides, some of the nicest boys I know are non-Catholics. How is our faith going to be known if Catholic young people can't date with those of a different religion?

✥✥✥✥✥✥

YOU know, Maisie, there are a lot of people who share your views. According to interviews and public opinion polls, a good percentage of Americans—Catholic and non-Catholic—feel that there are few hazards connected with mixed marriage. This is all the more startling because religious leaders, Catholic, Protestant, and Jewish, have constantly warned their flocks about the dangers of such unions. This raises the interesting question: Is anybody listening?

Let's look at the known facts about mixed marriage. Extensive studies conducted by sociologists show conclusively that mixed marriages are harmful to the faith of the Catholic party. Stated in broad figures, approximately 45 per cent of the Catholics involved in valid mixed marriages have either severed all connection with the Church or attend Church services very sporadically. Likewise, the religious training of children suffers in such marriages. A conservative estimate would be that roughly 40 per cent of the children born to such unions are either unbaptized, or are baptized in the Protestant church, or are baptized only, that is, they receive no formal instruction in the Faith. Finally, although a considerable number of partners join the Church before marriage, relatively few are converted during the marriage.

What are some of the sources of trouble in mixed marriages? First, it hinders the spiritual unity of the couple. The Catholic partner must pray alone, attend church services alone, approach the communion rail alone, and retain, unshared, a whole world of spiritual experiences and values. Second, there is lack of agreement concerning the religious training of children. Third, church loyalties in regard to time, interest, and money are divided and can lead to quarrels. Fourth, there may be rejection or positive interference from in-laws. Fifth, and most important, differences in religion produce basic differences in value systems which love cannot resolve. Catholics have distinct beliefs concerning the indissolubility of marriage, marital fidelity, the use of contraceptives, and so on. Although many Protestants hold these same values as *ideals,* the great majority feel that they can be ignored in exceptional circumstances. The Catholic partner can never agree to such an interpretation of divine teaching.

What about dating non-Catholics? The answer is simple. In the normal course of events, dating leads to courtship and marriage. If you wish to avoid getting involved in a mixed marriage, you must logically avoid dating non-Catholics. I realize that it is common to use the facile excuse that you are "only" dating, but where does one draw the line between dating and becoming emotionally involved or falling in love?

Once you have reached this stage, experience shows that it is not easy to break up.

This suggests one further point against dating non-Catholics. It always involves the danger of invalid marriage, that is, of attempting marriage outside the Church. Our studies show that somewhere between one-third and one-half of all mixed unions are invalid. No doubt, many of the Catholics involved in these unions started out by "only" dating non-Catholics, but the casual date became a "steady" and love followed.

Are you listening, Maisie? Or will you be one of the many thousands who complain, "Why didn't you warn us!"

Are Too Many Activities
Taking Parents Away
From Home Too Often?

How much time should couples devote to outside activities? I'm thinking particularly of some modern family organizations such as Cana, Pre-Cana, the Christian Family Movement, and so on. It seems to me that some of these movements are defeating their own purpose in taking parents away from home where they belong. There are so many extra-familial activities already claiming our time, why add some more?

⌇⌇⌇⌇⌇⌇⌇

YOU have a good point there, Katie. Modern life has become so demanding on our time that there is danger that the home will be reduced to little more than a hotel. Father is away several nights a week, mother has her meetings to attend, and even the older children's time is becoming increasingly absorbed in social, religious, and school affairs. When is the family ever home together? It is a basic law of social interaction that unless people are together and do things together, they soon lose their feeling of unity and communion. Besides, how can parents instruct, guide, and get to know their children if they are never home together?

This is sound reasoning. Does it prove your point against our contemporary family movements? I think we shall have to analyze the situation further before we can give an adequate answer. These are the points that must be considered.

First, parents have a serious obligation to instruct, guide, and supervise their growing children. In the modern world, this task is both more necessary and more difficult than in previous times. It becomes more necessary because a whole series of outside influences such as movies, radio, television, printed material, and so on, affect the child and frequently contradict parental teaching. It becomes more difficult because the parents must compete for time and interest with these influences and a host of others which take both parent and child away from the home.

Does this mean that parents should spend all the time possible with their children? In itself, this may not prove very effective. What the child needs is to feel wanted and loved, encouraged in his efforts, corrected when he makes mistakes, instructed and guided in meeting new problems, and supervised in learning to live with others. This requires understanding and time on the parents' part, but its effectiveness is not wholly dependent on the amount of time spent with the children. Intelligent guidance, not social retirement, characterizes the adequate parent.

Second, let's look at the family movements you mentioned. They have several pertinent features. First, they involve husband and wife as a couple, thus drawing them together in unity of thought and action. Second, they involve couples facing similar problems and seeking Christian solutions. Third, they are apostolic. They aim to strengthen and stabilize family life in contemporary society. This is a serious obligation which all Christians are bound to assume. Since Catholic families exist as a minority in our country, they need to join together, both in deepening their own understanding of marriage and in promoting this understanding among others. This is a task which they can and must perform if Christian family life is to flourish.

You know as well as I do, Katie, that there will always be some who will become absorbed in outside activities to the neglect of their parental obligations. Obviously, they are mistaken in their zeal. "One swallow does not make spring," as the old French saying goes. The efficacy of no movement can be judged legitimately on the basis of the few who happen to err.

Daughter Calls Parents
Old-Fashioned Concerning
Modesty in Dress

My 17-year-old daughter has just explained to me that I'm quite old-fashioned in my views concerning modesty in dress. She's been invited to an important affair and insists that the only "decent" thing to wear is a strapless formal—all the other girls are going to—so she says. I won't have any trouble handling this occasion; what I'm thinking about is the future. How can I help her acquire a balanced view toward modesty?

∽∽∽∽∽∽

I N ONE way or another, I suppose every generation of American mothers has been regarded as old-fashioned by its growing daughters. Changes take place so rapidly in our society that even the brief period separating mother and daughter suffices for the development of different attitudes and customs. The problem is felt keenly by the younger generation because they have such need to belong, to be like others in their age-group. This need stems from their desire for acceptance. Their individuality has not yet developed to the point where they feel secure enough to differ from their companions. Adolescent girls, in particular, because they are not fully aware of their femininity, resent some of its implications. As one young thing summarized it, "Almost everything I like is either immoral, illegal, or fattening!"

How can you help your daughter acquire a balanced view toward the virtue of modesty? First, remember that growth in modesty requires both knowledge and motivation. The regulations you impose are bound to be misunderstood and resented if your daughter does not understand and appreciate the principles and social facts which prompt you to make them. Second, training for modesty must go hand in hand with training in related virtues. Vanity, failure to acknowledge responsibility for the effects of one's actions on others, and even sheer laziness are factors to be considered. Third, because current social customs may run contrary to Catholic values, you must teach your daughter to think in terms of basic Christian principles. Catholic youth frequently feel penalized because of the demands of their faith. Teach your daughter to see the positive relationship between acceptable Christian behavior and her privilege as a follower of Christ.

What are the principles and social facts she should know? First, because modesty is essentially related to chastity, serving as its guard and protector, she must understand the Christian view of sex. This means that she will know and appreciate the relationship between her developing reproductive faculties and her role in marriage and motherhood. She must be made aware that her distinctive nobility as a feminine person is based on her capacity to share with God in the procreative act through motherhood. Thus she will come to know and appreciate the true source of her womanly nobility and attractiveness.

Second, you must show her how modesty is related to chastity. This means that she must acquire some understanding of the physical and psychological mechanisms of sexual arousal in herself and in the opposite sex. She should know that some actions are bound by their very nature to cause sexual stimulation, that others may do so under certain circumstances or for certain individuals. Hence she must view sexual stimulation as a normal process which she must regulate directly in herself and indirectly in her companions, to the extent that she avoids doing anything which would normally cause undue stimulation in others.

Finally, don't exaggerate, and don't try to frighten her. Acquiring a balanced view toward modesty is part of the normal process of growing up. Like all processes, it takes time. Remember, modesty is related to chastity, and your purpose in training for chastity is twofold: that your daughter remain virginal until marriage, and yet enter marriage with a mature, balanced view toward sex.

Is There Any Cure for Women Who Have to Nag All the Time?

Why do some women have to nag all the time? I have a fine wife in many ways. She's an efficient housekeeper— too efficient, perhaps—and she's a good mother. Yet she seldom lets up on me around the house. Her ability to recall the things I forget to do is remarkable. Every little thing starts her off. Is there any cure?

❧❧❧❧❧❧❧

WELL, you may recall that Shakespeare gave us one in his *Taming of the Shrew.* It was a "get tough" policy that produced marvelous results in the play. I have serious doubts that it would work very well off stage. In real life, one man does not write all the lines; and the plot, especially in marriage, has a way of developing which thwarts all predictions.

The problem of nagging appears frequently in marriage literature. Even the ancients recognized that a woman's tongue was her best weapon. We are told that the famous old Greek philosopher, Socrates, seldom stayed home because he feared it so much. He could spend hours skillfully arguing with men in the market place, yet he was no match for his sharp-tongued wife, Xanthippe. Down through the ages the

81

belief has persisted that some women are born to nag, and may the Fates help the man who marries one!

But all wives—perhaps most—don't nag. This should lead us to suspect that there may be sound reasons why some do. Before we can talk about a cure, we must discover the possible cause. Let's go over a few of them.

First, some women find frequent grounds for nagging because of their peculiar definition of the home and the role of housekeeping. Efficiency and order rather than family living comfort determine their outlook. The home and everything in it become a kind of show-piece, to be left clean and orderly at any cost. We might say that they value the house more than the home. From their viewpoint, husband and children are necessary but irritating disturbers of the peace. One has to keep them constantly in line.

Second, some husbands provoke nagging by their refusal to cooperate readily around the house. They are frequently late, they have to be called several times for meals, they keep postponing or forgetting necessary jobs around the house. Such tendencies exasperate most women and they set out to correct them. Husbands often consider these abuses as very minor affairs, forgetting that they may occasion serious inconveniences for their wives.

Third, in some women, nagging is a manifestation of personal frustration. They are dissatisfied either with their roles, their social positions, or the successes of their friends. They are not sure just what they want, but they are restless and unhappy, peevishly working out their discontent on those around them.

After thinking over your family situation, how do you diagnose the trouble? Is your wife the watchdog type, guarding the house from all disturbance? If so, you'll have to put up with some nagging, for this fixation is not easily cured. Are you being neglectful and uncooperative? Then the remedy is simple, and it's up to you know whom. Is the nagging merely a symptom of some deeper discontent? Then your diagnosis will have to go further. Maybe the daily routine and monotony of keeping house are hard on her nerves. Try taking her out once a week or more. Maybe the task of rearing children has narrowed her interests to the small circle of the family. Help her widen her view by getting her to go out and meet people in church, school, and social activities.

A nagging wife is made, not born. It is worth your best effort to see that this doesn't happen in your marriage lest the "angel in the house should become the devil in the kitchen."

Is It Important for
Marriage Partners to
Be the Same Age?

Is it very important for marriage partners to be about the same age? I'm 20 and Joe is 28. I think the world of him and I guess he feels pretty much the same about me. We've never thought much about our differences in age, but recently the girls at the office brought it up. They say the happiest couples are those about the same age. Is that true?

≈≈≈≈≈≈≈

THE first point to remember, Mabel, is that age is a relative factor. It is not how old you are, but what you are that makes for success in marriage. A good deal of nonsense has been written about the advisability of marrying someone your own age. This advice is based on the belief that adjustment will be more difficult if the spouses differ considerably in age. The assumption seems to be that biological age and adaptability in marriage are closely related. We have no good reasons to assume that this is true.

What is the over-all picture for age differences at marriage in this country? A reliable estimate would be that in about 10 per cent of the cases the bride is older, in somewhere between 10 and 15 per cent of marriages the couples are the same age, and in the remainder the groom is older.

85

In the majority of cases where age differences exist, the spread is between one and five years. The cultural heritage of a group more than anything else determines what its marital standards regarding age will be. In general, the groom tends to be older because he must be able to support a family before he can prudently marry.

In your case, Mabel, the age difference is somewhat greater than is usually found in our country. Does this mean that you and Joe will encounter special problems in marital adjustment? Let's look at the situation. Marriage means companionship and partnership in parenthood. It is not a static affair. In the normal course of events, you will move from the intimate two-in-oneness of early marriage, through the turbulent, busy years of childbearing and child rearing, to the serene companionship of old age. How will difference in age affect your relationships throughout this family cycle? Strictly speaking, age difference in itself will not be noticeable until the last stage in the cycle. Because women in our society tend to live longer than men and you are considerably younger than Joe, you can expect to outlive him by some years. Of course, this is no more than a statistical average. You have no way of knowing whether it will be verified in your case so that you would be foolish to worry about it at this time.

Your real problem is not difference in age but difference in character. Here you must ask the same questions about Joe at 28 as you would about Joe at 18. Is he responsible and capable of supporting a family? Is he domineering, stubborn, self-centered, and "set in his ways," or is he a good companion, showing respect for your likes and dislikes and willing to cooperate in making adjustments? Is he emotionally mature to the extent that he displays reasonable self-control and balance in meeting trying situations? Does he share your standards of value and agree with you on the things that are worth-while in life?

If Joe scores well on these counts, grab him! He's probably your man. The girls at the office may have your best interests at heart, but they are mistaken if they believe that age difference in itself is an important factor in marital happiness.

My Husband's Work
Requires Travel: We
Lack a Normal Family Life

My husband's work takes him from home most of the week. I don't have much trouble keeping busy because we have three children, aged five, four, and two. It does get lonesome at times and I miss his companionship. He says it's the work he can do best, that maybe he can get a job at the home office in a few years. I'm worried about our lack of normal family life. Aren't we losing something valuable?

≈≈≈≈≈≈

I DON'T have to tell you, Louise, that modern industrial society offers many jobs which place a heavy strain on family life. Employment which keeps the husband away from home for days or weeks at a time is bound to be trying for all members of the family. Such absences are perhaps most keenly felt in the early years of marriage when the children are small and their care confines you closely to the home. It would be ideal, of course, to maintain your little family circle always intact. The daily companionship of husband and wife in the home is one of marriage's most pleasing rewards. But men must make a living as best they can under modern conditions. Your husband's job is only one of many which may put some strain on family life.

89

What's the best way to handle your problem? First, it is not advisable to persuade your husband to change his job unless he can find other employment equally satisfying for him. He evidently likes his work and feels he stands a good chance to better his position if he stays with it. He may not find it easy to settle down in another line of work, so the decision to change jobs should come from him.

Second, although your companionship is restricted, it need not suffer in depth and quality. Learn to make the most of the time when he is home. Let him feel that he is very much a part of the family circle. If necessary, put off some of your work until later so that you can spend more time together. Keep him interested in what goes on around the home while he is away. Set up some regular custom of communicating either by letter or telephone while he is traveling. This may seem to be a small point, but in the long run it is not. The old saying "absence makes the heart grow fonder" seems to be based on wishful thinking. In real life, a sensible couple will make use of all practical means to maintain communication during separation.

Third, a problem to which you should pay considerable attention in your circumstances is your children's attitude toward their father. Because he is away so much, they will tend to focus their affection on you. This may be flattering and rewarding for you, but it is not healthy for anybody concerned. Children need both mother and father. With a little thought, you can easily bring father into the picture. Build up their expectations when you are expecting him home. Show him how to deal with them. Provide opportunities for him to be with them. Remind him how much he means to them. Suggest that he remember them with a little toy or trinket when he returns from a trip. In this way you can build him into the family circle and the family will grow around you as a couple.

Married companionship can take many forms, Louise. Some couples live together all their lives, yet never really get to know each other. Some, absorbed in raising a family and earning a living, seem to drift farther apart as life goes on. Yes, any husband and wife can lose something valuable in married life if they are not careful to grow together as a couple. Your problem is essentially the same as that of all married couples. Your husband's job merely requires that you take a different approach in meeting it.

Children Take Parents' Control for Granted. Do Yours?

My husband and I just can't seem to agree on how to raise our children. We have three, aged 7, 5, and 2. I was taught that too much restraint and discipline would crush their initiative. I try to reason with them, but must admit that it doesn't always work. My husband says you don't reason with children before they reach the age of reason, you tell them. Who's right?

※※※※※※

WHEN parents hold sharply opposed views concerning how to raise children, what was meant to be one of the chief blessings of marriage can destroy its happiness. The history of some marriages could be written: "Till children did them part!" Perhaps the problem is peculiarly modern because the past two or three generations of parents have been subjected to such a variety of theories about how to raise their children. Theory has run the gamut from putting children on a strict, practically adult regime to smothering them with love and permissiveness. Parents are warned that too much authority is harmful, that they should use a "democratic" approach. This leaves them confused since neither authority nor democracy is clearly defined in terms of everyday family living.

93

It may help you to reach an agreement with your husband about child rearing if you consider the following points. First, children are children, not adults in miniature. They are short on experience and long on energy. Consequently, you can reason with them only up to a point. At one time or another, all normal children are noisy, irrational, stubborn, mischievous, and rebellious. These are common moods of an emotionally healthy child. To treat them as developmental phases through which the child must pass undisciplined and the parents must suffer undisturbed is sheer nonsense. Part of the process of growing up consists precisely in learning to control these passing moods.

Second, you must look upon your children as part of the family; they are not the whole of it. They must learn respect for the rights of others, consideration for others' feelings, and cooperation as members of the family team. Because children uniformly start life as pretty much the center of things, they must be taught that there are others in the world. There is something absurd about parents who allow their undisciplined children to disrupt family order at will.

Third, there is a world of difference between love and overindulgence. Even young children are quick to exploit overindulgent parents. Since one of the hardest lessons in life is to learn to take "no" for an answer, you would be unfair to your children if you deprived them of the opportunity to learn this lesson in the home.

Fourth, you will put an undue strain on your children if you expect them to be able to make up their own minds and plan their own activities at all times. They lack the knowledge, self-control, and experience required for this. Hence they become restless, irritable, and peevish when you refuse to lay down regulations and enforce them. Children take parental control for granted. What upsets them is to be forced to meet problems and make decisons for which they are not yet prepared.

Fifth, growing up is a gradual process which requires growth and time. Your job as parents is to assist your children to learn the proper norms of conduct and to acquire the self-control needed to live up to them. This means instruction, encouragement, discipline, good example, and steady growth in assuming responsibility. Your children are not adults, but they are moving toward adulthood. You will not help them by treating them as if they were already adults. Now they need affection and the sense of being wanted. They also need instruction, firm discipline, and an opportunity to learn what it means to live as a member of a group. Step by step, as their experience widens and their self-control increases, you can teach them to rely upon themselves rather than upon you.

In this sense, all good parents finally work themselves out of a job! The point to remember is that it takes time.

Will the Coming of a
Baby Change Our
Close Companionship?

*The doctor has just assured me that I'm really pregnant.
My feelings are running between joy—maybe pride—and
regret. My husband and I have become such close companions since marriage that I'm wondering whether the
coming of a baby won't change it all. I've noticed that
some couples seem to lose their spirit of companionship
once children arrive. How can we prevent this?*

❧❧❧❧❧❧

I N MANY ways, Nora, your first baby will be your most
exciting and your most important. Its coming will mark
your entrance into maturity as a woman. It will also mark
the end of a definite stage in your marriage. The carefree
companionship of your early married life will become a thing
of the past. Like the courtship and honeymoon periods, it
was not meant to last, and like them also, it loses its significance when it is unduly prolonged. For marriage is a
dedication to the service of life, a partnership in parenthood.
You cannot experience the fullness of its companionship until
your love has become productive. Never will you feel closer
to your husband than on the day you can place in his arms
the child you have nourished and borne for him.

There is an old French proverb which says we reach each

new stage of life as novices. Pregnancy and the coming of a child are new stages in married life. Every couple faces them as beginners with much to learn. You are correct in observing that many couples seem to be separated rather than united by the coming of children. Why did their early companionship cease to grow as their marriage moved into maturity?

There are several possible reasons for this failure. It may be worth-while to review them briefly. First, some young brides regard pregnancy as a major illness. In the final months they become quasi-invalids, demanding attention, sympathy, and service. Most young husbands are not prepared for this outcome. They generally cooperate, of course, but it leaves them resentful. Some "invalids" even infer that their condition is primarily their husband's fault, and consequently he should be made to feel a little of their misery.

Second, some young mothers-to-be make the opposite mistake. They seem to regard pregnancy as their unique concern and possession. They reason that this is an affair which concerns only women; husbands don't want to be bothered about it, and besides, who's carrying the baby? This is a serious mistake, particularly during the first pregnancy.

Why leave your husband out of it? It's his pregnancy as much as yours. How can this experience unite you unless you help him share it with you, unless you watch developments and look forward to the great event as a couple? This is his initiation into fatherhood. Involve him in it from the start and it will draw you closer together each step of the way.

Finally, a word of advice for the future. A baby can be very demanding. The first one in particular can easily monopolize all of your attention. Never forget that you still have a husband. Some women become so completely absorbed in being mothers that they don't have time to be wives. The baby is only one member of the family, and as he grows, this is about the most important lesson that he'll ever have to learn. But some wives have to learn this too. The center of the family is not the child, rather it is the couple, united as two-in-one-flesh, embracing the child.

No, Nora, your new experience need not weaken your spirit of companionship. Share it at every step, and your feeling of unity will so develop in extension and depth that your present happiness will appear youthful and insignificant.

Do Differences in Nationality Cause Difficulties in Marriage?

Do differences in nationality necessarily create special difficulties in marriage? I never gave this problem a thought until I met Ann. She's third generation and thoroughly American. Everything was going fine until we announced our engagement. Now our families are bringing up all kinds of objections. We don't think they make sense, but we'd like to be sure. How do national differences show up in marriage?

～～～～～～

A S THE poet Walt Whitman wrote almost a century ago, "We are a nation of nations." Americans from different national backgrounds have been intermarrying throughout the history of the country. Today, many Americans can count a variety of national stocks among their ancestors. The history of the major national groups settling in this country tends to reveal the same pattern. On arrival they concentrated in more or less separate groups frequently clustered around their national parishes. Similarity of language, culture, and religion tended to hold them together for a time, but in the process of making a living their descendants gradually lost their national distinctiveness. The rate of change varied considerably among different groups. Furthermore, because they arrived at different periods, they now reflect different stages in the process of Americanization.

Intermarriage between the members of different national groups represents the final stage in cultural assimilation. When people are willing to accept marriage with the members of another group, it means that they no longer consider nationality differences important. In this connection, it is interesting to note that since the various national minorities in our country enjoy different social rankings, intermarriage with a member of one of these groups is frequently favored or opposed on the basis of this social ranking. It is not so much the character of the individual that is considered but the social esteem of the national group with which he is identified. Thus, opposition to an intergroup marriage may arise either because a minority wishes to maintain its national distinctiveness or because it considers other minorities to be inferior. Both these factors may be involved in regard to a given marriage.

This is the over-all picture, Tom, and I think you should keep it in mind when considering the opposition to your marriage with Ann. However, your question was focused more directly on your own marriage. Will you have to meet any special problems because of your differences in national background?

To answer this question you must determine to what extent you and Ann agree in defining family relationships. What does she expect of her husband and the father of her children? How does she define her role as wife and mother? Do you share her views in this regard? Nationality differences are important in marriage only to the degree that they represent incompatible ways of defining the statuses and roles of husband, wife and children in the family. If she has been trained to have one view of how the family should operate and you have been trained to have another, there can be trouble. Marriage is a partnership in parenthood. Because national groups may differ in the way they define acceptable marriage relationships and also the relationship between the individual couple and the wider circle of relatives, you and Ann should find out if you agree on these matters.

Hence, it is not the fact of nationality itself which matters. Rather, it is the possibility that different training and conditioning in the parental home may have given you different views concerning how your family should function. I think you must realize that this possibility exists in all marriages. Every husband and wife have been trained in somewhat different family backgrounds. Trouble arises only when these differences are not resolved and become elements of conflict rather than of completion.

Relatives and Friends
Say We Are Having
Children Too Fast

We've just had our third child in four years. We're healthy, happy, relatively free from debt, and quite contented with the way things are going. We wanted a family when we married and are grateful to God for giving us one. But others don't seem to look at it our way. Before the last baby arrived, female relatives and neighbors started a sympathy campaign for my wife as if she were the victim of some misfortune. I know they regard me as thoughtless and inconsiderate. Is there something wrong in having a family?

෴෴෴෴

YOU know the answer to that question as well as I do, Al. Your experience illustrates a peculiar confusion, if not hypocrisy, in the attitude of some modern Christians. Let's look at the facts. Marriage is a vocation designed by God to lead men and women to happiness and sanctity. Christ has raised it to a sacrament, thus making it a constant source of supernatural strength for the couple. It has a specific, primary purpose which distinguishes it from all other vocations. This purpose is to provide for the fitting procreation and education of children. Two conclusions follow.

First, husbands and wives are privileged to cooperate in the creative act of God by bringing children into the world, and with the redemptive work of Christ by rearing members of His Mystical Body. Second, since this is the meaning of their vocation, they will find happiness and sanctity in it to the extent that they help each other in living up to it.

This is simple Catholic doctrine, learned and accepted by all the faithful. There seems no good reason to presume that your female Catholic relatives and neighbors don't know it. Furthermore, marital relations usually form an integral part of a normal, healthy, young couple's life together. Representing a natural expression of conjugal love, they are closely related to the purpose of marriage both in terms of reproduction and the fitting control of sexuality under the conditions of cohabitation. Hence, complete abstinence, except for very special reasons, is neither easy nor to be recommended for long periods. We may presume that the normal adult female is not unaware of these facts of life.

Finally, it follows that under the circumstances, the only remaining practical alternative to bearing children in marriage is some form of avoiding pregnancy, the normal outcome of marital relations. Two general methods are available. One is the use of rhythm or periodic continence. To be morally justified, this requires considerable control and sufficient reason for using it. The other includes the various forms of artificial birth control. This method is always seriously sinful.

Now we may safely presume, Al, that your female relatives and neighbors are also well acquainted with these facts. We can only conclude, therefore, that when they strongly imply that you are having too many children, or having them too rapidly, they are either ignorant of Catholic doctrine and the facts of life, or they are subtly suggesting that you have recourse to prohibited methods of birth control. Of course they will pretend to be very shocked that we should draw such implications from their actions, but isn't it rather unrealistic to suppose that at their age they are just ignorant?

It may seem too harsh to call them hypocrites. Perhaps they are only extremely shallow Christians. At any rate, if children are a blessing of marriage, they should rejoice when you are blessed with them. If their coming seems a heavy burden under some circumstances, they should lend support and assistance as they are able. But there is no excuse for treating the young wife as an unfortunate victim and her husband as an inconsiderate brute. Such an attitude offers a disturbing example of the pervasive influence exercised by un-Christian secular thought upon some modern Catholics.

Don't let them upset you, Al. This is your marriage, rich in opportunities for happiness and sanctity, provided you follow the Creator's plan for it.

You Can and Should Regulate Your Children's Use of Television

We're having some difficulty making up our minds about the use of television in our home. They say that some of the programs children watch are not really good for them. This may be true, but I feel it's better than sending children to a movie where we have little control over what they see. Besides, children can learn a great deal from watching television, and it does keep them out of the way when I'm working. How should parents deal with this problem?

~~~~~~~~~

MOST modern inventions, whether the automobile, the movies, radio, or television, have created new problems for parents. I suppose our great grandparents had their parental problems, too, but they were clearly quite different. Radio and television are important because they enter directly into the family circle in the home. Since most of the programs they carry are designed for entertainment rather than education, they command a large audience among both young and old. Watching television, in particular, has quickly become one of our major national forms of diversion and information. It follows we can't simply ignore it or rule it out as harmful.

What can parents do? In the first place, you can regulate the amount of time that your children spend in watching television. Some parents appear childishly helpless here, protesting that their children won't obey them in this matter. Such a state of affairs is absurd, suggesting that parents have no control over their children in any important affairs. Of course, if children have been allowed to do as they please from the cradle on, it is not surprising that they will want to have their way in watching television. Mature parents will see to it that television does not interfere with their children getting the proper amount of exercise, finishing their homework, and helping with the assigned tasks around the house. This offers a much needed opportunity to teach responsibility, proper management of time, and self-control.

Second, you can regulate the type of program your children watch. This means that you must pay some attention to what is being offered. With a little effort you can come to know the programs which you feel are suitable for them. In this matter, as in so many others, you are personally responsible as parents. The fact that some programs are supposed to be designed especially for children does not free you from this obligation.

Third, you can teach your children to appreciate good programs. There are many ways of doing this. You can call their attention to such programs and stimulate interest in them by discussing, explaining, and showing the children where they can read about them when necessary. Above all, you can show your own appreciation for these programs by enjoying and sharing them with the children.

Fourth, as your children mature, you can use various programs to help them develop critical insight and a sense of values. Why do they like what they like? If the program offers something objectionable, do they detect it? Can they tell you why it is objectionable? In this way you can learn a great deal about your children's needs and outlooks on life. You can help them acquire the habit of judging things in terms of Christian principles. As you well know, young children can ask a thousand questions a day. While they are growing toward maturity, you must make use of all that they see, hear, and do to show them how they can reason through to the correct answers.

The most important lesson you can teach your children is this constant need to interpret life and the world of their experience in terms of Christian values. The use of television in your home offers a wide scope for teaching this lesson.

How Should Husbands and Wives Divide Authority in the Home?

How much authority should the husband exercise in the home? My wife and I work things out together well as a team. She runs the home and does much of the buying, while I earn the money. We agree fairly well in handling the children. This seems to work out all right, but lately I've read a lot of statements to the effect that modern men have made a mistake in giving women so much authority. What does it mean to be the head of the home?

✿✿✿✿✿✿✿

IT WOULD be easy to answer your question if terms like authority and headship could be meaningfully defined apart from the social situation within which they are exercised. Even a slight knowledge of different social systems reveals that this is not possible. Perhaps we can clarify the problem by starting with general principles and then proceeding to concrete situations.

According to Catholic teaching, husband and wife are absolutely equal as persons. They enjoy equal rights in what pertains to the marriage contract. However, because they fulfill different roles in reproduction, they have different roles in the family. The husband's headship must consequently be defined in terms of the common good of the family unit. In marriage, husband and wife unite to form a special society in which their sexual complementarity gives them different roles. The husband's authority, therefore, stems from and is limited by his role as protector and provider for the reproductive unit. It is not a privilege which he can use for his own interest. It can never legitimately extend beyond the purpose for which it was established by God, namely, the good of the family.

Inasmuch as all authority comes from God and God is Love, all authority exercised in His name will be characterized by love. But love is the gift of self. In exercising authority in the family, the husband gives himself to the family according to the qualities which God has given him as a male. Likewise, obedience is an act of love. In obeying her husband in the legitimate exercise of his authority in the family, the wife gives herself to the family according to the qualities which God has given her as a woman.

As a going concern, the family, like any other society, requires someone in authority. The husband's job as breadwinner normally places him in the best position to fulfill this function. When social conditions change, the manner and amount of authority he exercises necessarily changes. In American society, happy married couples tend to work out their problems together. Each contributes according to ability and past experience. Thus it develops that the mother makes most of the immediate decisions around the home, while the father makes the long range decisions and those pertaining to activities outside the home. As companions in a common enterprise, both should consult each other and lend mutual support, particularly where the children are involved.

What really counts in marriage is that both husband and wife work for the best interests of the family. As the chief breadwinner and provider, the husband has not only the authority but the serious obligation to plan for the long range welfare of his family. When he takes this obligation seriously, wife and children find little difficulty in looking up to him. Every normal woman is proud to have married a man capable of assuming responsibility.

I feel that much of this talk about authority is beside the point. The real problem is that too many husbands become totally preoccupied with their work or with outside activities and leave the entire task of running the household and caring for the children to their wives. If you and your wife have learned to work together as a team, so much the better. The main point is that you shoulder your share of responsibility in training, guiding, and directing your children. If you do this, you will be head of the family.

Why Is It Considered
Wrong to Date a
Divorced Person?

Why is it considered so wrong just to go on a date with a divorced person? If people are old enough to know their own minds, there's no reason why they can't go out together merely for entertainment. When they both recognize that there can be no thought of marriage, what's the danger of going out together once in a while? After all, divorced persons are human, too; they can't be expected to sit home all the time.

※※※※※※

WELL, Betty, I think you know the answer as well as I do, although you may find difficulty in facing it squarely. However, because a good number of people seem to share your views on this matter, it may be worthwhile to go over the situation in some detail. According to reliable estimates, between 700,000 and 800,000 divorced persons are being turned loose in American society every year. The majority of these eventually remarry and it appears that they do not necessarily remarry other divorced persons. At present the chances that a divorced person will marry are as good as, if not better than, the chances that a single person in a similar age group will do so.

117

The fact that the majority of divorced persons seemingly encounter little difficulty in finding suitable mates and eventually remarry suggests that such unions are no longer regarded with strong disfavor by the American public. Indeed, some commentators point to the high rate of remarriage after divorce as an indication of how highly Americans must value marriage. Although we have no complete data concerning the number of Catholics involved in divorce and remarriage, there is sufficient evidence to show that an increasing number are following the popular trend.

This does not necessarily mean that all such Catholics have completely rejected the Church's teaching on marriage. No doubt, some of them have. The majority, however, are conscious that in either remarrying or in attempting marriage with a divorced person they are living contrary to the divine law. They find themselves entangled in such situations because they have allowed themselves to fall in love under circumstances in which valid marriage was impossible.

As you see, Betty, this brings us to the subject of dating. Daily experience in this matter teaches a very simple fact. The association of adult males and females in the dating process easily leads to more or less conscious mutual attachment and eventually to that emotional involvement called love. When this happens, some couples convince themselves that their need for each other is greater than their need for God, so they enter a civil marriage. Others refuse to take this step and continue their frustrating association for years.

Nobody can deny that the lot of the divorced person in our society is very difficult. Since remarriage is impossible under the circumstances, he must seek happiness and fulfillment by heroically directing his energy and interests along other channels. This is an impossible task unless he faces his problem realistically and humbly seeks strength and motivation from prayer and the sacraments.

It should be obvious that you are not really helping a divorced person adjust to his difficult situation by accompanying him on dates. Moreover, you are not only running the risk of falling in love with him, but you are also seriously lessening your own chances of meeting a legitimate partner. It is easy to put up a smoke screen of excuses, rationalizations, and false justifications to soothe our consciences, but we don't destroy reality by our refusal to face it honestly.

No, Betty, you can't continue to date him if you wish to keep God's friendship.

What Can We Do to Modernize Our "Old-Fashioned" Parents?

My husband and I have an in-law problem in reverse. Our relatives don't interfere with us, but we'd sometimes like to change them! We both have parents who are second generation descendants of immigrants. They frequently embarrass us by their slips in grammar, their views on food, dress, marriage, family life, etc. We don't like to neglect them, yet they really live in a different world. What should we do?

~~~~~~~~

YOUR problem is what the social scientists call a culture conflict. When it occurs in the family, it means that parents and children have learned two different ways of life and consequently fail to agree. It has been common in our country because we are a nation of immigrants—only the Indians are really natives. Coming originally from many different nations and cultures, successive waves of immigrants brought with them their own diverse ways of life. Their descendants passed through, or are now passing through, the various stages of gradually abandoning the old ways and adopting the new. The speed with which the change is made varies greatly among different groups and among individuals within the same group. Some adopt new ways at once, some cling to

121

the old, only to see their children take up the new. The possibilities for conflict between generations must be evident.

In handling this problem, several points should be kept in mind. First, there is a tendency to consider what is old or different to be inferior to the new and familiar. This need not be true. There are many ways of preparing food, dressing, raising a family, and so on. Different cultures have worked out different ways of life. Who is to say which is superior? However, because most of the immigrant groups coming to America arrived poor—the rich usually don't migrate—their language and culture came to be considered socially inferior by those who had arrived before them. The terms *foreigner* or *immigrant* became synonymous with socially inferior, though in reality they mean only *different*.

Second, many of the immigrants and their descendants have been slow to drop their native language and culture, not because they are incapable of learning the new, but because they value their own. We may not agree with their attitude, but we certainly cannot question their right to it. Older people in particular find it hard to understand why they should change. They are proud of their native heritage, enjoy their own way of life, and believe we should accept them as they are. Some would even feel guilty of betraying what their forefathers suffered and fought for if they were to abandon their language and culture here.

Third, as members of our minority groups move into the social system, nationality differences gradually become less important. The process takes time, but we no longer feel the compulsion to "Americanize" everyone by force and brand all national differences as marks of inferiority.

Hence I feel you are being a little hard on your parents. Aren't you paying too much attention to non-important differences? Chances are they have made sacrifices and worked hard to give you an education. They are happy to see you get ahead in life. They cannot fail to be disappointed if the result is that you neglect them now. If you are ashamed of them, it can only mean that you still feel insecure.

Why not be realistic? They are your parents, to whom you owe love and respect. They have given you life and raised you—nothing will ever change that. They cherish their language and their traditions. Are these necessarily inferior? You say they live in a different world. In a sense, every generation does, but is it so different that love and sympathy cannot lead to respect and understanding?

The Right Approach to
Spending Money
for Children

How much spending money should we give our children? We have five, three boys and two girls, ranging from 6 to 15. Although we've managed to stay fairly well out of debt, by the time all the bills are paid and a little set aside for future schooling, there's very little left. Our children complain that others always have more spending money. This may be true, but we like to plan for the future. Are we being unfair to our children now?

~~~~~~~~

I THINK you realize that there is no simple answer to your question. Family sizes, incomes, social positions, and environments differ greatly. The sex and age differences of children must also be considered. Hence, more important than the amount of spending money is your children's attitude toward it and toward money in general. Attitudes acquired in childhood tend to endure throughout life. Your real problem is to teach your children the Christian attitude toward money and the things it can buy. If you neglect this, the amount of spending money you give them remains relatively unimportant.

A consideration of the following points should help you meet this problem. First, show your children that all blessings, material and spiritual, come from God. Teach them to have a deep respect and gratitude for the food, clothing, and home they enjoy. These are blessings which neither you nor they have wholly earned. God has granted us a rich country and prosperous times. Millions of others just like ourselves have lived and still live without enjoying them. Knowing this, we must regard even the crust of bread and the worn garment with reverence and gratitude. You must live and teach this lesson carefully lest our present excess blind you and your children to the true Source of these blessings.

Second, build up in your children a spirit of loyalty and understanding toward your family as a unit. According to their ages, children should be brought into your family council so that they can appreciate the over-all needs of the family, share in your concern over the budget, and participate in your plans for the future. This is a maturing process for growing children. It develops loyalty and legitimate pride in one's family because each child comes to think of himself as a member of the team. Some parents foolishly exclude their children from their councils in the mistaken belief that they will learn the hard facts of life later on. How can children acquire a sense of family unity and an understanding of the family's financial limitations if they are given no knowledge of the facts? Is it not unfair to make them wait until they are married to discover that the family budget must be balanced with money which they have earned?

Third, make an honest attempt to understand the spending needs of your children. These will vary with age and sex, but you can make a reasonable estimate if you take the trouble. To refuse all spending money may exclude the child from ordinary participation in his age-group. Under these circumstances, some children may even resort to dishonest means to obtain money. On the other hand, some children attempt to buy favor and friends with money. You must show them that this is the wrong way to retain friends. In general, if you take the trouble to understand your childrens' real needs and have taught them to think in terms of the family, you can handle the problem of spending money without too much difficulty.

Fourth, teach the spirit of sharing. Children are a strange mixture of generosity and selfishness. Remind them of the needs of others, and show them how, through making some small sacrifices, they can give something to charity. They are never too young to start learning this lesson.

Finally, help them to acquire a true sense of values. Teach them that happiness is based on a quality in the heart, not on an object in the hand. This lesson is learned slowly. Most generations have to learn it anew. Yet it is fundamental for Christians. Remember, Christ spent His whole life teaching it—from the poverty of the manger to the nakedness of the Cross.

May a Bride Continue
to Work Until the
Babies Start Coming?

Is it all right for a bride to continue working until the babies start coming? George and I were married right after he finished school, so we had no money saved up. I've been managing to handle my job and the apartment pretty well so far, and we do need the money. However, we're very anxious to make a success of our marriage, too. Am I endangering our future happiness by continuing to work?

❧❧❧❧❧❧❧

I KNEW this question would come up sooner or later! Frankly, the problem is so complex that no simple answer can be supplied. No two marriages are alike. What may prove harmful for one couple may draw another more closely together. This obvious truth isn't going to be much help to you in deciding what is best for your marriage. Perhaps I can help you reach a prudent decision by recalling a few principles and facts relating to your problem.

First, it is not a mere question of work. In every society, most wives have worked and worked very hard. The modern problem is their employment outside the home. Changes in the social system have so modified the functions of the household and the position of women that past patterns are no

129

longer entirely applicable. Over half of the modern brides have been employed before marriage. Many see no good reason why they should not increase the family income by continuing to work after marriage. In most cases it is not a question of a career but of more or less temporary employment.

Second, marriage is a partnership in parenthood. When you enter marriage, you dedicate yourselves to the service of new life. Conjugal love is by its nature productive and creative, seeking to extend and fulfill itself in a child. This is the normal way that marital happiness grows to maturity. It follows that anything which interferes with your partnership in parenthood offers a threat to your happiness.

Third, parenthood involves a necessary division of labor. During the childbearing and child rearing period the wife's energy and interest must be focused on the home if she is to perform her task adequately. It follows that the family must live primarily on the income supplied by the husband. Under ideal conditions, therefore, marriage should mark the beginning of this division of labor, and the family's standard of living should be based on the husband's earning capacity.

In the light of these facts and principles, I think we can safely draw the following conclusions concerning your problem. First, your husband should agree to your employment outside the home. Second, you must both agree that your job is temporary, that is, you will quit working when it becomes clear that you are going to have a baby. Third, from the beginning, you will base your standard of living on your husband's earnings. Whatever income you make should be used to pay past debts, buy furniture and other extras, or be put aside to cover expenses related to having a baby. This point is very important. If you start marriage by basing your standard of living on your pooled incomes, pregnancy will represent a threat to your standard of living. You may thus tend to postpone it or, if it happens, you may consciously or unconsciously resent it.

Finally, your job must not prevent you from taking care of the home. This is not easy, since you are really holding two jobs. Young couples who must rush off to work in the morning and return tired at evening frequently come to look upon the home as little more than a hotel. Their companionship suffers and they miss the deeper meaning of domestic partnership.

If you feel you should hold your job, you had best set a definite date for its termination, and then stand by your decision. Like most other families, you will always be able to use more money, but you married because you wanted **happiness.**

Is There an Ideal
Length for the
Engagement Period?

Is there an ideal length for the engagement period? Rose and I have been engaged for one year, and we're not sure when we'll be able to get married. We've been told that the Church discourages long engagements. What is considered to be a long engagement, and what does a couple do if conditions do not permit marriage for the time being?

✹✹✹✹✹✹

BEFORE answering your questions it might be well to point out that the term *engagement* is used rather loosely in our country. At one time it represented an external rite and a formal promise to marry, pronounced before witnesses such as the relatives or a representative of the Church. The Church has a formal engagement or betrothal ceremony although changing social conditions cause it to be used rather infrequently. At present the formal rite usually consists in the giving of the engagement ring, and its wearing signifies that the couple have exchanged promises to marry. Strictly speaking, the external rite is not necessary and is sometimes ignored. The essential point is that the couple have come to a definite agreement that they are to be married.

The Church has no explicit, general position on length

of engagement. The conditions associated with courtship and the entrance into marriage differ widely in various cultures so that clear-cut norms of universal applicability cannot be devised. Whenever rules pertaining to length of engagement are advanced, therefore, they have specific social situations in mind and must be interpreted accordingly. In general, religious leaders have two concerns in mind when formulating such rules. First, they wish to assure the stability of marriage. Second, they wish to guard against violations of chastity.

For example, in a society such as our own where young people are expected to select their future mates through the dating and courtship process, religious leaders oppose hasty marriages. Only if they have associated for some time can future partners learn something about each other's character and personality. Since the engagement period normally represents this intimate learning experience for the couple, religious leaders are uniformly in favor of such a period.

On the other hand, since this engagement period involves strong emotional attachment, together with more or less frequent and prolonged displays of affection, it presents considerable moral danger for the couple if marriage is postponed for a long time. Obviously, the danger will depend on the temperament of the couple, the frequency with which they associate, and the self-restraint which they exercise in showing affection.

Hence the ideal length of engagement cannot be defined as a matter of months or years. It should be long enough for the couple to become thoroughly acquainted. Under normal circumstances, one year should suffice for this. It should not be unduly prolonged, since sexually mature partners normally find it difficult to restrain their impulses under conditions of continued intimacy. Thus, an engagement of two years or more would normally involve special problems for one partner or the other.

You ask what is to be done if marriage still remains impossible. If this is really the case, and you should make sure that it is, you had best try to determine precisely when marriage will be possible. If this can't be done after two years of engagement, why continue the affair? If the date must be postponed to a fairly definite time in the future, then you must regulate your present relationships accordingly. This requires sincerity and honesty with yourselves for you will need to keep your feelings under constant watch. In general, avoid frequent and prolonged physical displays of affection. After all, you may as well learn at once that they are only one way of showing love.

We Have Difficulty
Finding Suitable Friends
in Our Neighborhood

We've just moved into a new neighborhood and find some difficulty in meeting suitable friends. Many of the couples our age seem to have a different outlook on life from our own. They drink more heavily than we are accustomed to doing, many of their parties start on Saturday night, and their whole system of values seems different from our own. So far we've hesitated to mix with them. Are we being prudish?

～～～～～～

THERE'S an old saying, "you can judge a man's character by the company he keeps." This saying applies to couples, also. Whether it is because "birds of a feather flock together," or because frequent association breeds conformity, the fact is that you cannot mix freely with a group for long without acquiring some of their attitudes and standards of conduct. Few of us like to be thought different. It sets us apart from the group, and we want to belong, to be accepted and treated as one of the "crowd." Besides, we have been taught from our youth to be "team players," to go along with the group even though we do not agree with them or particularly care for what they want to do.

The prudent selection of friends is particularly important

for young married couples. We live in what is called a pluralistic society. Stated in briefest terms, this means that Americans do not agree on values, norms, and standards of conduct. This lack of agreement is most marked in regard to sex, marriage and the family. Although in theory there exists a rather broad, vague acceptance of the traditional Christian view in these areas, in practice we find little agreement or uniformity. The reason is, of course, that the American people no longer agree on the origin, nature, and purpose of man. Hence they cannot agree on the nature and purpose of marriage or on the standards of conduct which should regulate family life. Instructed Catholic couples have clear ideas about the meaning of life and consequently about the nature and purpose of marriage and the family. Although this provides for some minor differences in behavior, the general standards of conduct are rather clearly defined.

As you have remarked, some of the couples you've met seem to have a different outlook on life from your own. Their standards of conduct are different. If you reflect that you are living in a pluralistic society, these differences should not surprise you. What you may find difficult to understand is that other Catholic couples should have such different views from your own. Are you being prudish?

The answer should not be difficult. Are their views and practices opposed to, or likely in the long run to prove harmful to, your spiritual growth in your marital vocation? The aim of this vocation is the mutual development of your happiness and sanctity as partners in the family enterprise of child-bearing and child rearing. Although there is room for considerable variation in the way this is achieved, certain attitudes and standards of conduct are clearly incompatible with it. If other couples cherish these, you had best check them off your list of prospective friends at once.

In choosing your intimate family friends, it is important to remember that once you have entered a group, it is frequently difficult to withdraw. Particularly if they live near you, it is embarrassing to find excuses for not continuing to associate with them. Unless you have strong convictions, you will probably follow the path of least resistance and gradually adopt their views and practices. The urge to conform is strong in the best of us.

Recent studies of stable families showed that they tended to be self-protective in selecting family friends. This is to say, they chose to associate only with other families that were stable and shared their views. It was found that stable families followed this pattern even when they moved to other neighborhoods or cities.

There's a wide difference between being prudish and being prudent. Even though it takes some time, select your friends with care. Remember, you are judged by the company you keep because you tend to become like the company you keep.

What's a Reasonable
Curfew Time for
Teenagers Today?

What's a reasonable time for teenagers to get in at night? Our two oldest children are now in high school, and this question keeps coming up constantly. It was discussed at one of our PTA meetings, but opinions varied so much that most of us came away more confused than before. Are there any reliable norms parents can follow in this matter?

∽∽∽∽∽∽∽

A EUROPEAN observer has remarked somewhat maliciously, perhaps, that American parents spend half their time worrying about when their children will turn in, and the other half about how they will turn out. He also commented on how well American parents obey their children. There is more than a little truth in these observations. Some parents seem to be afraid of their job, almost as if they doubted their right to instruct, guide, and supervise their children.

It should not be too difficult to work out the basic norms concerning the time teenagers ought to get in. In fact, it is a matter of rather elementary arithmetic. The average teenager requires at least eight hours' sleep a night. Individual needs may vary, but the average is a safe norm to follow.

141

Now if you add in the time required for dressing, washing, morning prayers, and eating an adequate breakfast before starting for school at eight or eight-thirty in the morning, you will find that bedtime should normally be around ten o'clock on school nights. There's nothing mysterious or difficult in figuring this out. Indeed, if an individual child requires more sleep, has special responsibilities around the home in the morning, or must travel a considerable distance to school, the time for retiring may have to be even earlier.

Furthermore, since the evening is the only time normally available for doing homework, pursuing special interests such as hobbies, practicing music, and so on, spending some time with other members of the family, and getting needed relaxation after a long and busy day, it should be evident that going out on school nights must be limited. This also is a matter of simple arithmetic. No matter how you plan it, there are only twenty-four hours in a day. Since time is limited, first things must come first.

Week-end evenings, when the problems of homework and sleep are not so pressing, the question of going out and of a reasonable hour for getting in appears somewhat different. Young people have social obligations and should be offered an opportunity to fulfill them. Teenagers enjoy going out at night just as you parents do. They like parties, traveling with the gang, and the reputation for being a good sport. Learning to mix socially with others is an essential part of the process of growing up, but it may cause you parents some worries.

What can you do? First, you should know where your children are going, with whom they are going, and what they intend to do. Some silly parents think that to require this information constitutes an invasion of their children's privacy. This is absurd. Because parents are responsible for their children, they must have this information. Second, you should know when the affair is expected to be over and how your children intend to come home. In terms of this information, you can then set a reasonable hour for getting in. This hour should be reasonable, that is, certainly not later than one o'clock under normal circumstances. Finally, you should train your children to notify you if they will be late or if they need your help.

You may feel that I am overly strict in this matter of going out and getting in. My position is based on common sense and simple arithmetic. Your children have a job to do: grow up in good health and get an education for life. Precisely because they are not adults, they cannot be expected to manage this alone. In all fairness to them, your job as parents is to see that they get an even break.

My Wife and I Can't
Agree on the Kinds of
Friends to Cultivate

My wife and I can't seem to agree on the kinds of friends we should cultivate. We come from somewhat different family backgrounds. Neither of us gets along very well with the other's former friends. She wants me to drop most of mine because she doesn't approve of some of the things they do. I think this is unfair. I tell her she can have her friends and I'll have mine. What's wrong with that?

❧❧❧❧❧

I THINK you realize, Bill, that the answer to your question calls for the making of a few necessary distinctions. Marriage is a partnership based on companionship. When you marry, you agree not only to establish a family but to face life together as two-in-one-flesh. The married couple are one, joined by a sacramental contract and the deep mystery of marital relations in a companionship for life. Although marriage does not deprive you of individuality, it does oblige you to think always in terms of your partner. This thinking together includes friends as well as other family relationships.

This is the over-all picture, but, as you suggest, reality isn't quite so simple. Former long-standing friendships tend to persist and to be valued. If husband and wife cannot agree on these, trouble is bound to arise. Let's look at the situation a little more closely and perhaps we can see in what direction the solution will lie.

First, it should be obvious that a married couple should have some friends in common. If they are to be real companions for life, they must learn to play together as well as work together. Indeed, a great part of their entertainment and recreation should be shared as a couple. The habit of doing things together starts with courtship. It should continue throughout marriage if marital companionship is to mean anything in the couple's lives. Some men apparently forget this. They expect their wives to remain at home taking care of the house and children while they enjoy the companionship of others. In some societies this is an accepted pattern. For various good reasons, it is not the American way of doing things.

Second, both husband and wife should take for granted that their partner may wish to maintain some friendships which may not be interesting to them. Opposition to this may stem from two sources. They may really feel that their partner's friends are not good for them and their marriage. Undue drinking, gambling, and questionable association with the opposite sex may be occasioned by such friendships, and the spouse may rightly object to their continuation. On the other hand, opposition may stem from over-possessiveness and the desire to have the partner entirely to oneself. Some spouses are suspicious and jealous of all friendships in which they do not share. Some resent the enjoyment which their partner apparently receives from them. This attitude does not spring from the desire for true companionship but rather from selfishness or the wish to dominate the partner.

In seeking a solution for your case, Bill, ask yourself the

following questions. Have you cultivated a group of friends which you and your wife enjoy associating with as a couple? If not, you had best start finding some, for something has been wrong with your attitude toward companionship. Do you object to your wife having some friends which you do not particularly like? If you honestly feel that these friendships are not harmful, you have no reason to object. Does she object to your friends? Ask yourself if their company may not be incompatible with your present role as husband and father.

Finally, does your wife seem selfish and over-possessive? Some women—and men—are. On the other hand, she may only be asking for an even break in companionship. The important point for your future happiness is that you start making friends together as a couple. If you do this, the few friendships you may wish to maintain separately will seem relatively unimportant.

I Am in Trouble
and Don't Know
Where to Turn

Please help me out. I'm desperate and don't know where to turn. Here's what happened. I'm a senior in high school and about six months ago I started running around with a boy a little older than myself. My folks didn't like it but most of the time they didn't know where I was. Now the doctor says I'm pregnant. Jack wants to elope although I don't think he loves me any more. We're both scared because my Dad has an awful temper. What can we do?

~~~~~~~~

THESE next few months are not going to be pleasant for either of you, but don't complicate matters by doing something rash. What you need now is a clear plan of action. Let's look at your situation as it really is. In the first place, you are carrying a new life within you. Although you did not want it, this little life came into being because of your activity and the creative act of God. Its future now depends upon you. It has every right to protection and love. You must cherish it as a marvelous, though unwanted, gift from God.

Second, forget this nonsense about elopement, even if it were possible. We can't correct one mistake by making another. It seems quite clear that neither of you is prepared for marriage, nor do you appear to be really in love. Hence, don't let anyone talk you into getting married as if this would be an easy way out of your troubles. Young people in your condition are often so frightened and ashamed that they will do anything their parents desire. Embarrassed parents sometimes push them into marriages which have little chance to endure. Marriage is a sacramental contract. It was not designed to cover our mistakes.

Third, you need personal guidance and counsel. Go directly to your pastor, or your regular confessor, or to some priest that you know, and tell him your problem. If you live in a city where an office of Catholic Charities is located, you may prefer to consult one of their counsellors first. At any rate, you must get the advice and help of someone who will know what to do.

Your parents must be informed, of course. Since you appear to be very much afraid of your father's reaction, it may be well to have the pastor or social worker assist you here. When faced with this situation, experience shows that parents react in many different ways. We would expect them to be hurt, embarrassed, and uncertain of what steps to take. Usually when the first shock is over, they are willing to follow the priest's or the social worker's advice. Because you and Jack are relatively young and obviously not prepared for marriage, this advice will run along the following lines:

A hospital or some similar institution will have to be contacted and arrangements made for you to go there in due time. If at all possible, this institution will be located in another city and you will leave home before your condition draws public notice. You have a right to secrecy in this matter and it should not be too difficult to find some excuse for your absence during this period. When your baby arrives, it will be adopted by a happy couple who have been carefully selected by a reliable social worker. This arrangement is best for the child because it has a right to the love and security of a stable home. Under the circumstances, you cannot offer this.

One final word of advice. At present you feel as though your life is in ruins. Truly, you have made a serious mistake, but your whole life lies ahead of you. Tell God that you are sorry you have displeased Him and then face the future with courage and hope. Remember, life moves on and time heals the deepest wounds. In a few years you will look back upon this whole affair as a bad dream. You are now learning some things about life the hard way. Accept this lesson, not in bitterness, rebellion, or despair, and don't waste your time looking for someone to blame. Fix your eyes on the future. It will be what you make it.

My Divorced Wife
Remarried. Where Does
That Leave Me?

My wife and I were divorced six months ago after being married for nearly two years. She wasn't interested in having a family and insisted on holding her job after marriage. Our pastor tried to help but got nowhere. I've just heard that she has remarried. Where does that leave me? I'm 26 and have my whole life ahead of me. I've already discovered how difficult it is to live alone. What can I do now?

≈≈≈≈≈≈≈

IT WON'T be much consolation to you, Jack, I know, but every year around 800,000 men and women find themselves in your predicament because of divorce. According to reliable estimates, the majority of them eventually remarry, as your wife has already done. If they were validly married in the first place, they are not capable of contracting another real marriage during the lifetime of their former partner, no matter what that partner may do. As you well know, their attempt to marry again is not a marriage before God. They are living together merely with state or civil permission. They cannot receive any saving grace through the sacraments. They are living at odds with God and with their own consciences.

As a Catholic, you recognize these facts, but as a normal adult male living in modern society, you are beginning to realize that you face tremendous difficulties. There are many reasons why this is true. First, you were trained and grew up with the expectation that marriage was to be your vocation in life. Your outlook, habits, education and work were more or less closely related to this expectation.

Second, although your marriage was apparently not a happy one, you did acquire some of the habits and experiences normally associated with married life. This implies that you now probably have a better understanding of what a successful marriage could mean in your life. In this respect, your problem differs from that of the normal unmarried male.

Third, most of the strictly social activities in modern adult society are organized around and on the basis of the couple or family. This means that you will find it difficult to participate in them as a single person.

Fourth, frequent association between a man and woman of marriageable age easily leads to mutual attraction and love. As a result, you cannot safely trust yourself to go on dates as an unmarried man could. You may argue that there's nothing wrong in dating a girl only once, but the number of available respectable girls is limited, and you would soon find you were dating the same girl more frequently.

Hence, we can only conclude that you are going to face frustration of your hopes for marriage, added difficulty in controlling your desire for affection and sexual experience, and considerable restrictions on your social activities. How can a normal man handle this situation? Let us be frank and realistic. You need heroic virtue if you are to persevere.

How do you acquire this? In the first place, you have the highest motives both in terms of saving your soul and guarding your peace of mind. You have the firm conviction that you are living in friendship with God and according to His law. Second, you need divine help. God offers this to you through prayer and the sacraments. You would be foolish if you thought you could handle this problem alone. Third, you must use common sense in organizing your life. This means that you will be honest with yourself in avoiding keeping company with the opposite sex. You will be tempted to fool yourself here, but look at the experience of others. It also means that you must find some activities which will be worthwhile enough to take up your time, energy, and interest. Some men find this in additional schooling, or by engaging in charitable and religious activities which are sufficiently important to require their best effort. There is generally work of such nature to be done if one has an eye for it.

I agree with you, Jack, this is no easy program. Remember, the stakes are high—your own self-respect and peace of soul. The civil law allows you to follow the crowd, but you must always end up by living with your own conscience —and with God.

The Best Way to
Handle Curiosity of
Young Children

Our three youngsters, aged 5, 3, and 14 months, are teaching my husband and me a great deal about children. At times we're not sure of the best way to handle a situation. What do you do when your five-year-old uses really bad words picked up at play? What about some of their games involving sex ideas? Are all children curious about themselves and others? When do they learn modesty?

❦❦❦❦❦❦

YOU obviously have three normal youngsters. They're setting out to get acquainted with themselves and with the world about them. The energy and speed they display in their desire to learn may dismay and surprise you. Everything is new to them, yet they are born explorers, tireless in asking questions, seeking new experience, and showing off what they have learned. Their persistence may wear you down and their curiosity may become a nuisance, but they're out to find the answers.

In handling the puzzling situations which may arise at these early ages, there are several points you should keep in mind. First, since sex and other bodily functions are normal human phenomena, they fall within the range of children's

157

curiosity and must be explained accordingly. This means they may make some interesting discoveries about their own bodies and have some understanding of how they differ from the opposite sex. They may even show curiosity about older people. When answering questions, remember that all facts are pretty much on the same level for children. Their interest will be superficial, temporary, and changeable unless some unexpected reaction on your part focuses their attention on some special area.

Second, do not project your adult feelings, knowledge, and attitudes into their questions or actions. They are children, not grown-ups. Their curiosity is that of a child rightfully wishing to know, not that of an adult seeking evil. Even when they do things which would be wrong for an adult, you should recognize that these actions both in their nature and in their meaning are quite different for the child.

Third, it follows that the best way for you to deal with such situations when they arise is indirectly. There's nothing to be gained, and a great deal of harm to be done, if you appear shocked or start scolding them as if they were adults. This can only serve to focus their attention on an area which normally would not interest them for long. Hence your aim should be to direct their attention along other lines by giving them something more interesting to do.

Fourth, modesty comes with age. The two- or three-year-olds who shed clothes with gross abandon in the summertime develop a keen sense of privacy a few years later. The same holds for their unabashed use of toilet words, bathroom curiosity, and so on. Children do grow up, and you will notice the change as they gradually realize that they are real, independent persons with a private life all their own.

Finally, growing boys in particular do pick up an amazing

vocabulary at times. Unfortunately, they frequently learn it from grown-ups whom they may admire, so that they feel big in using it. It's best to show neither amusement nor shock when this occurs. Simply tell your youngster that there are many kinds of words having many different meanings, that you and most grown-up people know all these words too. This approach tends to take the excitement out of such words, so that he generally stops trying to upset you with them. There's not much fun in using "shockers" that don't really shock.

My Husband Has
Started Drinking Too
Much for His Own Good

My husband has started drinking too much for his own good. He always drank some, but lately it is excessive every week-end. My children are afraid to bring their friends home because we never know what condition he'll be in. So far, it hasn't interfered with his work. When I talk to him about it, he always insists that I exaggerate. He says he can take it or leave it, and nobody is going to tell him what he can do. Is there any way of showing him how wrong he is?

❧❧❧❧❧❧

I WISH there were some simple answer to your problems. Drunkenness has strewn the pages of history with the wreckage of human lives and happiness, yet we know relatively little about its cause and its cure. Students of the problem usually distinguish between drunkenness and alcoholism. They define the alcoholic as a person whose heavy drinking not only gives rise to serious life problems but appears to be an addiction which he is incapable of mastering without outside help. He may protest that he can take it or leave it, but in reality, experience shows that he is unable to stop drinking for good unless he is willing to accept help from others.

161

Plain drunkenness, on the other hand, is defined as a strong habit rather than an addiction. Like other strong habits, it can be overcome by the individual drinker if he really wants to do so. In this sense, it is something like the habit of smoking. Although not many habitual smokers do quit, they are able to do so if they really try, as happens every day when doctors order it. In some individuals, the habit develops rapidly into an addiction; in others, it may remain no more than a strong habit all their lives.

If your husband is an alcoholic, as defined above, he needs competent outside help. Not much can be done for him until he is willing to call in the doctor, the priest, the psychiatrist, or Alcoholics Anonymous to help him out. Since most drinkers resent outside help until they've "hit the bottom," their lot is a sad one, indeed.

Let us suppose that your husband is not, or not yet, an alcoholic. What's the best way to deal with him? Well, I think that you have learned from experience that nagging doesn't help much. In his better moments, try to get him to see how unfair he is to his children. Some men will make sacrifices for their children that they will never make for their wives. It will be helpful here to get him interested in the children's growing needs and welfare. Some wives make the mistake of taking over the entire task of rearing the children, thus relegating the father to the mere role of breadwinner. This makes it easy for him to assume he's doing all that is required provided he keeps his job.

If his drinking has suddenly increased, try to find out what may be the reason. Is it added pressure at work, little peace at home, or ill-chosen companions? Perhaps you can find out what is causing him to turn more frequently to drink. At any rate, your best move is to attempt to bring him more completely into the family circle. Build up his self-respect, his feeling for the children and their feeling for him. Try to go out together as a couple or as a family as regularly as you can. Finally, help him to make the spirit and practice of his religion more active in his life through prayer and the sacraments. This should be done for its own sake, not as a "cure," since he will obviously resent the implication he needs such help.

Since these few observations can have only limited value, I suggest you write for a book like Father John Ford's *Man Takes A Drink* (Kenedy & Sons, New York), or Marty Mann's *Primer on Alcoholism* (Rinehart Co., New York). They will help you understand the problem and how best to deal with it. Remember, your problem is not: Who's wrong? but: What can we do about it?

How Old Should a Girl Be Before She Starts Dating?

How can I convince my parents that I'm old enough to go on dates? Although I'm 16, they treat me like a child. All the other girls my age are allowed to go out several times a week. How can I meet people if I seldom go on dates? My parents are kind but old-fashioned. They say there'll be time enough for more dates later on. Don't you think they're too strict?

~~~~~~~

YOU have a real problem, Janie, and I don't find it hard to understand how you feel. Every girl desires to be popular. It's normal to want to have dates and to have fun with those of your own age. You feel all the more restricted because "all the other girls your age"—you really mean some of the other girls, don't you?—are allowed to date freely. This seems quite unfair to you because you naturally like to think of yourself as one of the group.

Why do you suppose your parents take the stand that they do? You're sure they love you and want you to be happy. Do you feel that they are so "strict" because they are old-fashioned? Let's take a look at dating from their point of view. Maybe they have something on their side. After all, being "old-fashioned" or "new-fashioned" are loosely defined terms. The "old" need not necessarily be bad, and the "new" need not be the best.

Your parents are probably opposed to dating on two counts. First, they feel that you are now preparing yourself for life so that your interest and energy should be centered on getting an education and developing your talents. Frequent dating takes your mind from this task, and though they want you to be happy and have a good time, they feel that you should do so with them and with your girl friends.

Second, they believe that the type of association with the opposite sex which we call dating has a definite purpose which need not be your primary concern at your age. Dating is a process by which you get acquainted with eligible boys and eventually select your future marriage partner. Since you are clearly too young to be thinking seriously about marriage, they feel that you are too young to go out on frequent dates. Although dating is "fun," it also involves moral dangers which they feel you will be able to meet better when you are more mature.

Do their objections have any value? The first one certainly has. At present you have an opportunity to get an education and to develop your talents. The way you do this will pretty well decide what kind of woman you will be in your future life. If you waste this time, what will you have later on? You probably want to marry some day. What will you bring to marriage? The memory of youthful popularity or a balanced, mature personality?

Your parent's second objection is based on experience. Although you and the boys that you would date are far too young to think about marriage, you are physically mature enough to have to think about your feelings and emotions. You may find it difficult even to imagine that these would ever get out of control. That's because you have never experienced their strength in yourself or in others. It's not that you would directly intend to do anything wrong, but once you meet somebody that you like very much, you have no reason to believe that your reactions will differ from those of any other normal girl. Your parents know this and feel that they have no right to expose you to such dangers before you are more mature.

I know, Janie, growing up seems to be a long process. You are impatient to act like an adult. But why not take things one step at a time? Then as life unfolds, you will be really prepared for each new venture. What about the other girls? Well, they're not adults either. In allowing them to act as if they were, their parents are merely closing their eyes to the facts of life. Do you think this is fair?

Mother-in-Law Moved
in on Us. What Can
I Do About It?

We have been married six years and everything was going well until his mother came for a visit and just stayed on. She's a widow and claims she has no money. Her daughter will have nothing to do with her. I don't mind having her here but lately she has been making insinuating remarks about my family background, my housekeeping, and even my friendliness with the neighbors. I don't want my children listening to such remarks. My husband is afraid of her. What can I do?

∞∞∞∞∞

I FEAR your guest has already tarried too long, Marge. You are not going to gain very much by allowing the situation to continue longer. When two women are in competition for the control of one defenseless male, the situation can get pretty rough. Once the battle starts, no holds are barred. It will be of little avail for you to submit meekly or to strive for peaceful co-existence. Your mother-in-law is evidently out to strengthen her position and weaken yours. She is not likely to be discouraged by what she will interpret as weakness on your part.

I must confess, Marge, I'm a little hesitant to take up a problem dealing with mothers-in-law. Sad experience has taught me that every attempt to do so arouses a hue and cry right across the country. Evidently, mothers-in-law are on the defensive and are in no mood to be studied. I had best make my position clear from the start! Frankly, I feel that mothers-in-law are just like any other mothers—no better and no worse. The only difference is that the in-law situation offers more frequent opportunities to show up their good points and their bad. If they are really good mothers, they will become good in-laws. If they have weaknesses, certain in-law situations will bring them out clearly.

Now that I have made myself clear on that point, let us look at your problem. First, for the time being, let us suppose that your mother-in-law has no money and is really incapable of earning her own living. Under these circumstances, it seems clear that her children have the obligation to help her in so far as they can. It is equally clear that all her children, both sons and daughters, share this obligation. Some parents thoughtlessly settle on one child for emotional or financial support. This is unjust and can have serious consequences for that child's later life.

Second, it is easy to understand that your husband feels he is in a difficult position. He recognizes his obligations to you, yet he fears to offend his mother who probably has a sharper tongue and has the benefit of long years of experience in learning how to deal with him. Caught in this situation, most men tend to do nothing. In the vain hope that things will turn out all right in the end, they try to placate both sides.

Third, it follows that you must take the initiative. In a sense, you will have to give your husband an ultimatum: does he want you or his mother? This sounds harsh, but experience shows there is no other way of dealing with the situation. You cannot fulfill your role as wife and mother if present conditions persist. They are not going to change by themselves. The head of the family must act. When it is put squarely to them in this way, husbands realize that they can avoid the issue no longer. With a little planning and perhaps some sacrifice on all sides, provision can be made for supporting the trouble-maker without running the danger of breaking up the family. In the long run, it will be cheap at any price.

In dealing with similar cases, Marge, I have found it is always better for the wife to put her cards on the table. Otherwise she runs the risk of losing the respect of her husband and children and may be tempted to retaliate by becoming as vicious as the one she is fighting. I think you had best make your position clear right now.

Should High School
Seniors Own
Second-hand Cars?

Our oldest son, who is a senior in high school, has been begging us to get him a car. He says there are a lot of cheap second-hand cars on sale and he's willing to use all of his allowance to pay for the cost of running one. We've let him use the family car rather frequently, but he wants one of his own to take care of and tinker with. Is it wise to get him a car now or should we wait until he has started in college?

≈≈≈≈≈≈

I THINK it is safe to say that few modern inventions have done more to modify our way of life than has the automobile. Americans have never been a people to stay put. They have been on the move since colonial days. In the last two generations, cars have stepped up the amount and speed of that movement beyond all expectation. They are so much a part of the American way that we can't imagine what life would be without them. Serving as a means of transportation, communication, and entertainment, they have greatly modified traditional family life—to say nothing of what they have done to the family budget.

It is only natural, therefore, that cars present an attraction and a challenge for young Americans. To youth they offer the prospects of freedom, independence, prestige among one's age group, and a feeling of maturity which are hard to resist. As parents, you should have no difficulty in understanding and sympathizing with your son's desire to own a car of his own. He would not be a typical American boy if he didn't.

But sympathy and understanding alone won't solve your problem. In this matter, as in so many others, you have one basic question to ask yourselves: What will best prepare our son for his role in life? This is the inescapable obligation which you assumed when you placed the act which gave him life. Your chief concern, both in fairness to him and yourselves, is to see to it that he reaches manhood fully prepared to take his place in life. He's not going to thank you later on if through weakness or misguided kindness now you fail to protect his best interests.

What does a car have to do with all of this? Well, it shouldn't be difficult to figure out. Your son has a full-time job as a student. If he hopes to get anywhere in school, his interest and energy must be applied to his studies. Of course, if he's not a moron, he can manage to get by with a minimum of study, but he'll pay for his neglect throughout college and later on in life. It should be obvious he doesn't want a car just to keep in the garage. He wants to use it. But a car is a heady possession for a youngster. No matter what promises he makes, it will inevitably consume more of his interest and time than he can now afford. Are you being fair to him if you put this unnecessary obstacle in the path of his development?

Although they should know better, many parents seem to forget that their son's future success depends largely on the quality of formal training he receives in school. "Education" in America is a broad term often meaning little more than exposure to learning. If the child has not been taught to make present sacrifices in terms of future gains, if he does not receive intelligent encouragement and support from his family circle, the vague belief that education is good will not carry him far through his course of studies.

As the ancients put it: "Learning maketh a bloody entrance." The job of being a student is not an easy one. Naturally, young people seek distractions and escapes. Now that the opportunities for formal education have become so common, it is high time that both parents and students recognize that there is no short cut to learning. Don't let your son have to find this out too late.

And lest I forget, give your son a real break—don't let him have a car in college either!

What to Do if
Your Partner Seems
to Be "Playing Around"

My husband has me worried. Last week I found signs of lipstick on his handkerchief and we had an awful quarrel. Now he claims that he did this only to make me angry. I don't like to be suspicious, but I'm terribly upset. We have two young children and I'm worried about the future. Do you think he still loves me?

≈≈≈≈≈≈≈

FIDELITY is so intimately connected with marital love that I can well understand why you are worried. One of the characteristics of love between man and woman is its exclusiveness. When a couple are in love, two is a crowd, and three becomes one too many. The marriage contract sanctions this exclusiveness, for it prohibits not only adultery but all misplaced affection for a third party. When some modern couples claim that they don't care too much about what their partner does when he is away from them, they are merely indicating that they don't care very much for each other in the first place.

I have called attention to this point because some married people try to justify their actions by saying that strict fidelity is old-fashioned. They pretend to be opposed to adultery but claim they see nothing wrong in "playing around" a bit.

177

I don't have to tell you how shallow this attitude is. Your problem is how to deal with it. We may as well be realistic. Your husband isn't fool enough to put lipstick on his handkerchiefs merely to make you angry. You can safely presume it got there in the normal way. It may have resulted from a casual date, an office party, or even more or less of an "affair." What can you do about it? Well, there are several points to consider.

First, your husband may be immature. Some men grow up slowly—if at all. Their "play-boy" attitude is really an attempt to feel important and appear a man of the world. Modern society offers them many opportunities, and they use them.

Second, your husband may associate with a loose crowd that sometimes involves him in situations which he would ordinarily avoid. He means well but plays along with the gang.

Third, he may be carrying on with a definite third party. She may be using him, "making a play for him," or merely having some entertainment at his expense.

What can you do? First, it won't help much to show you suspect all his actions. He knows that you know and violently disapprove. Second, don't "throw it up to him" constantly. Men hate to be nagged even when, or especially when, they are guilty. Third, try to increase your feeling of partnership by keeping him interested in the children. Go out together as often as you can manage. Be careful about your appearance and your moods when you are with him. In a sense, you may feel that you are competing with outsiders. This may be true, but you are playing from a strong position provided you don't weaken it by becoming hard to live with.

You are wondering whether he still loves you. Of course, I can't answer that, but if experience teaches anything about such cases, I would wager that he does. As a wife you may find it difficult to understand how he can love you and still play around. Well, some immature husbands apparently can for a time until they find themselves. You were in love when you married, and now you have the added bond of children. Be your best self and you will continue to hold his love.

Finally, do not neglect prayer and the sacraments. Let religion draw you together and strengthen you as a couple. What God has joined together, no man can put asunder— if you stay close to God.

It Pays to Know
What Really Lies
Behind Lovers' Quarrels

How normal are so-called lovers' quarrels? Chloe and I have been engaged for nearly a year and we intend to be married in two months. Lately we haven't been hitting it off together very well. She says I'm over-serious and a worrier. I feel she's been over-protected and is a little spoilt. I'd like to make definite plans for the future, only she won't bother with them and we quarrel. Is this serious?

≈≈≈≈≈≈

BY A lover's quarrel, people generally mean a game of much-ado-about-nothing carried on pretty much for its own sake. It starts over some little misunderstanding or pretended neglect and ends just as easily. Your quarrels obviously stem from a different source. I wouldn't hazard a guess about the seriousness of your quarrels on the basis of the scant information offered here. However, it may be possible to help you clarify your situation by offering a few observations.

In the first place, marriage is a serious affair. It implies more than mere companionship. When they enter marriage, husband and wife dedicate themselves to the service of new life. This means that they are willing and prepared to assume the obligations related to childbearing and child rearing. Hence marriage requires an economic foundation, division of labor, mutual service and support. Both husband and wife must contribute the best that they have to make the family enterprise succeed.

You are apparently the type that likes to have things planned well in advance. You find security in order. Since marriage is a serious affair, you'd like to look ahead to see that all will run smoothly. You probably don't enjoy doing things in a last-minute rush or waiting until the future is upon you before you move.

Chloe obviously doesn't share your zest for planning ahead. You infer she's somewhat like the flowers of the field —unsolicitous for the morrow. This may be due to her family background and training. Some people think it is the hallmark of femininity to be entertainingly impractical. It is up to men to be provident and practical.

Try to answer these two questions: First, are you perhaps overly concerned about the future, anxious to plan it out in every detail? Is it possible that Chloe senses this and is reacting to it now? Second, does Chloe know the full meaning of marriage? Has she given any indication that she is willing to cooperate in shouldering its obligations when they arrive? She may be the type of woman that accepts things quietly and unhesitatingly when they occur. Perhaps she feels ready for marriage and merely wants to take things as they come.

If you conclude that you have irritated her by being overanxious about your planning, or at least, that she will cooperate fully with you in assuming the obligations of marriage when they arrive, your quarrels probably aren't very serious. On the other hand, if her objections stem from her unawareness of what married life implies, if she shows no inclination to face the facts of life realistically and practically, then you two are headed for trouble. Common sense suggests that you can't start a serious life partnership on that basis, and you would be foolish to think that the situation would change once you were married.

There are many kinds of quarrels. Some are silly, some are harmful, and some help to clarify human relations. The point to be looked for in a quarrel is what really lies behind it.

Modern Society Places
a Heavy Burden on
Some Catholic Couples

How much longer is the Church going to ignore modern living conditions? Most of her rules on marriage and the family were developed when people lived in a rural society. As it is now, couples who try to live by these rules find it practically impossible to get ahead. Just about everything they earn goes to raising a family. Why must sincere Catholic couples be shackled by an outmoded set of rules?

〰〰〰〰

THIS is a tough indictment, Ted, but I know that there are others who feel as you do about some of the Church's doctrine on marriage and the family. There can be no doubt that social conditions have changed. Most of Western society has moved from a primarily rural to an industrialized urban way of life. Some of the social changes accompanying this shift have not proved beneficial to family life. Poor and unsanitary housing, unemployment, inadequate wages, industrial accidents and sickness, insecurity because of total dependence on the pay envelope, these, and many others, have created serious problems for the family.

Furthermore, when production is centered in the shop or factory, not the home, children cease to be productive. They

185

become "mouths" rather than "hands," as in a rural society. At the same time, since the wife can now enter the labor force only by working outside the home, the process of bearing and rearing children also prevents her from increasing the family income by holding a job.

Finally, in American society, dating and courtship patterns promote early marriages, thus increasing the likelihood of numerous children. On the other hand, the American standard of living is geared to the small family. Many couples solve this dilemma by the use of contraceptive birth control. The Church teaches that this is seriously sinful. Here lies your complaint against her "outmoded" rule.

Now who made the laws concerning birth control? I shall answer this question by asking another. Who created man "male and female" and endowed human nature with sexual faculties by means of which man is privileged to cooperate with the Creator in bringing forth new life? It was God. In giving man reproductive faculties, the Creator thereby decreed the laws which govern their proper use, for these laws are based on the nature of things as God made them. How do we know the nature of things? By studying their operations.

Now if we analyze the reproductive system we see that in it men and women carry the co-principles of life. But neither life nor the co-principles of life are under man's direct dominion. They pertain directly to the Creator. Hence, man cannot use sex primarily for his own pleasure but only according to the purpose which God gave it. This means that if man chooses to make use of sex, he may not interfere with the normal physiological process which his act has initiated. Whether conception then follows or not is not in his power to decide. To interfere with the natural process by using contraceptives would be to act contrary to right reason, for he would then be both willing the reproductive act and not willing it at the same time. It would be seriously sinful because he would be usurping God's dominion over the co-principles of life.

This is the basis of the Church's teaching concerning birth control. It is founded on the unchanging nature of man, not on the nature of any social system, rural or other. It follows that the Church cannot do otherwise than teach what she does. If there is any change, it must be made in the social system. No one denies that modern society may place heavy burdens on some Catholic couples. The basic question is, should we direct our criticism against the evils and shortcomings in our social system or against the Creator of human nature? Remember, there is a hierarchy of values in life—"Seek ye first the kingdom of God." Modern man is not the first to have sold his birthright for a mess of pottage.

Should You Send
a Daughter to a
Non-Catholic College?

My wife and I are having our first major quarrel. She wants to send our oldest daughter to a non-Catholic college because the daughters of some of her friends are going there. She argues that the girl has a good Catholic training and will profit by studying with those in her social class. I'm a self-made man and don't know much about girls' colleges, but I've always wanted our children to study in Catholic schools. Perhaps higher education is different. Do you think my wife is right?

❧❧❧❧❧❧❧

THIS is one question I can answer directly. No, Bill, I don't think your wife is right. In fact, I rather suspect she knows better herself. There are plenty of Catholic colleges where your daughter can study with girls in her "social class"—whatever that class may happen to be. Would I be hitting very wide of the mark if I characterized your wife as a bit of a social "climber"? She would not be the first "mobile" Catholic to regard her religion as an unfortunate hindrance to social advancement. Such Catholics frequently try to gain acceptance by soft-pedaling their religion. They assure you that they are good Catholics, but—

There are many reasons why your daughter should con-

189

tinue her education in a Catholic college. In the first place, her understanding and appreciation of the Faith should keep pace with her intellectual development. The religious training she has received thus far is necessarily based primarily on memory, habit, and routine. In college she should deepen her religious convictions by gaining a more intellectual grasp of the reasons for the Faith she practices. To stop her religious education now, while she continues to advance in other fields of learning, is bound to leave her an unbalanced, insecure Christian. Catholicism is more than a set of religious practices learned in youth; it is an interpretation of life which must give meaning to each new experience, intellectual or otherwise.

Second, associated with this lack of positive religious training at a non-Catholic college is the danger of undermining what faith your daughter now has. Granting that her religious beliefs may not be attacked directly, much of what she learns will be presented and interpreted in a different frame of reference. When religious values are rejected, other values based on different principles tend to replace them. Almost without perceiving it, the student finds that human nature, man's purpose and destiny, are being studied and explained within a "scientific" framework which leaves no room for religion. Instead of offering an interpretation of life, religion is relegated to the unscientific realm of myth and emotion.

Third, the atmosphere of a non-Catholic college obviously can offer little support for a Catholic. The entire "climate of opinion" offers little encouragement for the practice of the faith. Young people in particular are highly sensitive to this influence for they desire to "belong" and to be one of the group.

Finally, most of the young men your daughter will meet are probably going to be non-Catholics so that there is every likelihood that she will become involved in a mixed marriage. There is no need to review the problems such marriages face. Is this the future you are planning for your daughter?

No, Bill, your wife is not right this time. If you have your daughter's real happiness at heart, you will insist that she attend a Catholic college. Of course you don't like to argue with your wife, but this is one time you have no choice. As head of the family you have the obligation to guide and protect your children. It will be no excuse to say that you tried but your wife wouldn't listen. After all, you are the head of the family, aren't you?

The Decision to
Use Rhythm Should
Not Be Made Lightly

My husband and I are wondering about the advisability of using rhythm. We have had four children in fairly rapid succession and feel that a break of a year or two would prove beneficial for both our health and our finances. We've heard so many conflicting opinions that we're not sure what to do. Could you give us some advice?

❧❧❧❧❧❧

THE decision to use rhythm should not be made lightly. Besides medical and moral considerations, it involves a choice between different family values. Perhaps I can help you arrive at a prudent decision by pointing out the essential factors which enter into the total picture.

First, there are medical considerations. This is the realm of the doctor. I merely point out that you will need the advice of a competent physician at least in the beginning. The method of computing the various periods is somewhat complex, and you will probably need his assistance if you wish it to be effective.

Second, there are moral considerations. These can be broadly summarized under three headings. First, you must both agree to the practice. Second, you must both be capable of using it without putting yourselves in the proximate danger

193

of sinning against chastity. Third, you must have sufficient reason for using it. This latter point has been the source of some disagreement. Fortunately, Pope Pius XII has clarified the Church's official doctrine on this matter. He points out that couples who make use of their marital rights have a positive obligation to provide for the propagation of the race. They may be excused from fulfilling this obligation either temporarily or permanently if solid reasons of a eugenical, medical, social, or economic nature indicate that this obligation does not bind them in their circumstances. However, if without such reasons, they should make use of their marital right throughout marriage and yet always deliberately avoid pregnancy, they would be sinning against the very nature of marriage.

Third, even apart from moral considerations, the decision to use rhythm involves a choice between different family values. Children are one of the great "goods" of marriage. As a gift from God, they are a noble and an ennobling blessing. Marriage is a partnership in parenthood. The fulfillment and sanctification of the married couple is found primarily in childbearing and child rearing. This does not mean that a couple should have as many children as they are physically able to produce. The chief purpose of marriage is the propagation *and* education of children. Childbearing and child rearing go together, and as the Pope has pointed out, child-rearing is the more important of the two aspects. Hence, the ideal family size is that number of children which the couple can bear and raise to Christian maturity. Since the family does not exist in a social vacuum or in an ideal order, this number will vary with the condition of the couple and the circumstances within which they have to raise their family.

Hence, the use of rhythm always implies a sacrifice. The

blessing of another child is postponed or avoided in order to secure some other good. The only other good which could reasonably match this blessing is the good of the existing family. By this I mean that postponement or avoidance of a possible future pregnancy can be considered beneficial only if it enables the existing family unit to achieve its total purpose more adequately.

In making your decision, then, you must weigh all of these factors. If you both agree to practice rhythm and honestly feel that you are able to use it, considerations of health and finances offer you *moral* justification to employ it for purposes of spacing. But you are not interested only in avoiding sin. You seek the best that your marriage vocation can give. In using rhythm you are restricting your privilege of cooperating with God in creating new life, and with Christ in building up His Mystical Body. On the other hand, you must prudently consider the long-range, total good of your existing family. Think on it prayerfully, and, if in doubt, consult your spiritual director.

How Long Should
a Girl Wait for a
Marriage Proposal?

*How long should a girl wait for a proposal to marry?
I realize this sounds as if I were desperate. Well, I'm not.
I just wonder whether Fred and I are getting any place.
We've been dating for about the past 6 years. Every
time the subject of marriage comes up, he has some
excuse. Should I drop him?*

〰〰〰〰〰

I WONDER if you realize, Ellen, that your Freddie boy
is not an uncommon type. You're quite right in asking
whether six years isn't long enough for him to make up his
mind. They tell me that in times past, fathers used to have
an effective way of handling such situations. After a young
man had started calling steadily at the house for a time,
father made it a point to meet him and ask whether his
intentions were serious. This generally separated the men
from the boys because if marriage didn't follow after a
reasonable time, father had to be reckoned with. This seems
a little unromantic, but it apparently worked out all right.
Great grandmother got married, didn't she?

Times have changed, and now we have to deal with
Freddie. There are several reasons why some men continue

to date a girl for years without proposing marriage. Let's see if we can discover what may be tying Freddie's tongue.

First, some men are so attached to their mothers or both their parents that they never think seriously of separating from them. They date for the sake of entertainment or as a matter of course, yet they have no serious intentions. Some parents, particularly if they are financially dependent on their sons, are quite proficient in keeping marriage out of the picture by playing up this attachment. Even when there is no question of financial support, some "moms" refuse to cut their sons loose, and they have been known to suffer sudden heart attacks if sonny threatens to leave them for another woman.

Second, some men are afraid of responsibility. They like their freedom and are never quite ready to assume the obligations of marriage. Obviously, they lack normal masculine drives, but we must take them as they are. Like those in the first class, they use dating for selfish purposes. They are exploiters.

Third, some men find it difficult to make up their minds. When faced with a major decision, they see so many pros and cons that they escape by finding excuses for avoiding the issue. They are drifters, hoping others will make their decisions for them, yet usually accepting the consequences once they are made.

Does our boy Freddie fall into one of these classes? If he's "mom's" boy, give him back to "mom" at once. You'll never really get him from her anyway. If he's a dodger, let him keep his freedom. He won't stay tied for long even if you managed to catch him. If he's the hesitant type and you want him, make up his mind for him. Maybe that's all he's waiting for.

At any rate, don't waste any more time on Freddie. Either he sets the date or drop him. Even though you have no other prospects in mind, you will gain nothing by continuing to date him. In fact, as long as you associate with him, there is likely to be no other prospect. Come to think of it, wouldn't it have been better if six years ago somebody had made Freddie declare his intentions?

Why Are the
Problems of Family
Life Always Publicized?

Why is it that only the seamy side of modern family life comes in for treatment? We expect this from newspapers and magazines, but this seems to be the fashion also in sermons and lectures. There are thousands of Catholic couples earnestly striving for perfection and sanctity in married life. We're not counting the cost. All we want is to do what is right. We're not asking for praise, either, but we feel one should keep the records straight!

❦❦❦❦❦❦

I RATHER fear you have a point here. Perhaps because deviation appears to be more colorful and exciting than normalcy, speakers and writers find it easier to discuss it. Vice seems to intrigue the imagination more than virtue. Did you ever meet a gossip who just couldn't wait until she had told you about a good deed somebody had done?

On the other hand, sermons and lectures may tend to concentrate on the "seamy side" for two reasons. First, it is felt that greater effort should be expended on the one that is lost than on the ninety-nine who are saved. Unfortunately, as you may well point out, the "one" isn't listening. Second, it takes much greater insight into human nature and the spiritual life to discuss sanctity than sin. I suspect that both of these reasons are operative in furnishing the basis for your complaint.

Yes, there are thousands of splendid Catholic couples earnestly striving for perfection in their vocation. They aren't complaining about the sacrifices associated with leading Christian family lives in the modern world. Rather, they look upon their faith as a genuine privilege, a divine gift in which many of their contemporaries have not been granted a share, a precious treasure which gives meaning and purpose to their marriage and family life. Like other American couples they are trying to get ahead and to raise their standard of living, but these aims are kept carefully subordinated to their true purpose in life.

It is easy to understand that such couples grow somewhat weary of constant accusations or insinuations of worldliness, secularism, materialism, and so on. Particularly since these terms are seldom defined in relation to their daily lives and the problems which face them, they come away from such sermons and lectures perplexed and not a little resentful.

For their consolation, these couples should know that their daily lives are a source of real encouragement to their spiritual leaders. Priests and religious who have the privilege of knowing and working with them closely are truly edified and inspired by their Christian lives. This is as it should be, of course. We are all members of one Body in Christ. Every member, by giving practical testimony of his love for Christ, strengthens and inspires all the others to love Him more.

It should be a source of further consolation for such couples to know that their family lives of Christian piety and happiness have great apologetic value. They offer concrete proof that fidelity to God's laws produces stable, happy marriages and that these laws are not impossible of fulfillment in the modern world. In the long run, virtue is more attractive than vice. As the consequences of the rejection of God's plan for marriage become more apparent, thoughtful people are bound to be attracted by the wholesome family life exemplified by faithful Catholics.

Yes, there are many faithful couples. They do not make the headlines. Perhaps in their zealous preoccupation with warding off the wolf from the fold, some shepherds may forget the size of their flocks. Yet the faithful know that their names are written in the Book of Life. Surely, this keeps the records straight!

We Want a
Large Family; Our
Youngest Is Subnormal

We've looked forward to having a large family, but now our youngest child shows signs of being seriously retarded mentally. The doctor says it's too early to predict the full extent of the trouble. My wife is heartbroken and has started worrying about having another child. I don't know what to think. Why do such things happen?

~~~~~~~

FEW things cause parents more suffering than the discovery of some serious abnormality in their children. The child is an extension of themselves. They look forward with pride to its normal development. The discovery that their fond hopes will not be realized is both painful and humiliating. Almost unconsciously they ask why this should happen to them. Is it the result of heredity? Have they somehow failed in the past? What will others think? Why is God sending them this cross? Will they have to put the child in an institution? Will a specialist be able to help?

These are normal questions under the circumstances. No doubt, you and your wife have already raised them. Your hearts are heavy. You are probably more puzzled and worried than you want to admit. What should you do?

First, you must examine your own attitudes and feelings.

205

This child, like your other children, is a blessing from God, an immortal soul confided to your loving care and destined for happiness in Heaven. The Creator knows that it will require special protection and care, but it is His child as well as yours. Accept it humbly and gratefully from His hands as a sacred trust confided to you. It would be unbecoming as Christians to feel ashamed of this gift. Neither should you indulge in the strange superstition that God is punishing you. The child is a blessing, only an un-Christian attitude can make it appear anything else.

Second, you must be practical and realistic. There is nothing to be gained by running to a dozen different specialists. Put the child under the care of a single competent one, and follow his advice. He will tell you what to expect and how best to serve the child's needs. Later on, special training may be required. Unfortunately, some parents of retarded children, either through false pride or poor judgment, do not give them the opportunity to develop their full potential. Such parents would be surprised to see the gains their children would make when placed under expert care. At the same time, they would probably learn that many other parents face the same problem that they do.

Third, there is the question of another baby. Is it advisable to have another child? In answering this question we must remember that mental deficiency may be inherited, or congenital, or acquired through injury or disease. Only if it is inherited is there the possibility that a future child may be affected. Although modern science has made considerable advances in the study of hereditary factors, specialists in the field are still unable to make reliable predictions about future births in many cases. In general, if your other children are normal and there exist no cases of mental deficiency in your immediate families, there is little likelihood that your future children will be affected. Of course, if you have serious grounds for doubt, consult an expert, since the ordinary physician cannot be expected to give advice in so specialized a field.

You ask why such things happen. You really mean, why does God permit them to happen, don't you? Parents ask the same question at the death of a child. The answer is the same. We do not know the mind of God. His ways are not our ways. But the Christian knows that "for those who love God, all things work unto good."

Childless Couple Is
Bothered by the
Remarks of Others

We have been married for almost nine years and the doctor feels certain that we will never have any children. We have accepted this as God's will, but apparently others don't see it that way. Time and again, my husband and I have been subjected to cruelly insinuating remarks, as if we were guilty of some crime. Why should good Catholics take this frightfully unchristian approach? Aren't there many other couples in our situation?

∾∾∾∾∾∾

YES, there are and perhaps always have been childless couples in every society. Sometimes God has worked a miracle to bless such couples. For example, the Old Testament tells us that He did this in the cases of Abraham and Sarah, of Anna, the mother of the great prophet Samuel, and of Zachary and Elizabeth, the parents of St. John the Baptist. These are exceptional cases, of course, but they show that the problem existed even among God's chosen people.

In our society, it is estimated that about one out of every ten couples remain childless in spite of their fondest hopes and desires. Modern medical experts are devoting a great deal of attention to this problem. Just last year they held an international congress in Rome where their work was highly praised and blessed by Pius XII in a special audience. According to medical opinion, there are many possible reasons for childlessness, some known and some to be discovered. Contrary to traditional belief, doctors now tell us that it results from some condition in the husband about as often as in the wife, while some cases apparently result from a combination of various factors.

As you say, you accepted your childlessness as the will of God. What bothers you is the attitude of so-called "good" Catholics toward your situation. Obviously, they are well enough informed to know that all cases of childlessness are not voluntary. Why do they maliciously insinuate that your case is?

The answer is simple, though distressing. I suppose there is no clearer evidence of Original Sin than the persistent tendency of people to see evil rather than good in their fellowmen. This tendency is strong in the best of us. Unfortunately, it is allowed to develop unrecognized and unchecked in some. Such people regard themselves as the self-appointed guardians of their neighbor's morals. You just can't win against them. Like sharp-eyed harpies they size up the bride-to-be to see if she may be pregnant; if no children arrive after marriage, they nod knowingly toward the drugstore; if pregnancies occur frequently, they leave no one in doubt concerning what they think of the husband.

There isn't much one can do with these holier-than-thou critics. A sermon doesn't touch them because they spend their time applying it to their neighbors. Scripture says, "Judge not, and you shall not be judged," but they seemingly feel so self-righteous that they do not fear the judgment. The real tragedy of their situation is that they will never confess their sin because they refuse to recognize it.

You'll just have to ignore their remarks. On the other hand, God has work for you to do. Although He has not blessed your marriage with children, He offers you other opportunities to serve Him. Use your time and talents to serve Him in your neighbor. God's children have many needs. Like the priest and the consecrated religious, your parenthood need not be any less real because it is wholly spiritual.

Budget Battle Distresses
Father of
Large Family

We're constantly in debt. We have four children and are expecting a fifth. I'm holding a pretty good job but as my wife says, it seems that there's always too much month left over at the end of our money. After wrestling with our bookkeeping the other night, I felt like the fellow who told his family, "Well, I've finally balanced the budget, but one of us will just have to go!" Any suggestions?

❧❧❧❧❧❧

YES, Al, I have a few, but let me start out by telling you that there are a good number of young couples with growing families who find themselves in pretty much the same boat today. There's only one employer paying them wages, but there's dozens of trained experts to tell them how to spend it. Overcoming sales-resistance has been developed into a fine art, although we must admit that in many cases there isn't much resistance to start with. Just as insurance companies have found that some families are sickness or accident-prone, others appear to be debt-prone.

However, I don't intend to dismiss your problem that superficially. Let's face the facts. Anyone trying to raise a fair sized family under modern urban conditions is bound to

213

meet financial problems unless he's in the upper income bracket. The constant effort required to balance accounts normally proves difficult enough; once you allow debts to pile up, you place a persistent strain upon yourself which can seriously affect your marital happiness.

Now if you look around, Al, you will find couples who manage to retain financial balance on the same, or even less, income than yourself. Perhaps we can learn something from studying how these successful couples manage their affairs. What do they do?

First, they keep some type of budget. This does more than tell them where their money has gone. It sets up a hierarchy or scale of future expenses, with those items which are absolutely necessary for the family's existence at the top. These must be paid first, and only if some income remains over, can other expenses be incurred. As some cynic has remarked in this connection, "A budget is a way of balancing your net income with your gross habits." Some couples don't get around to paying essential family expenses until they discover they have already spent their month's income on less necessary items. Further, if you keep a budget, you will soon discover that you are spending many small amounts carelessly. A little here and a little there bulks much larger than you realize if you keep no account of it.

Second, they shop carefully. They watch the papers for bargains, and when they intend to purchase a large item, they wait for a sale, or consult friends who may give them a lead or help them obtain a discount. This is routine procedure today, since it is an open secret that only the inexperienced pay the regular list price for most major items. Further, they know that cash purchases readily receive a discount—

buying on an installment plan is expensive, no matter how you figure it out.

Third, they carry some form of family health insurance, either in connection with their job or in some acceptable group health insurance plan. All families require some medical care, but under present conditions, the cost is almost prohibitive if the family is not covered by insurance.

Fourth, they have learned to do without. Every item of expense represents a choice when income is limited. Since they can't buy everything they want, they learn to weigh one item against another. In a sense, Al, families like your own have many of their choices made for them. Once they choose the joys and blessings—and the costs—of having a family in preference to selfish childlessness, many of their future decisions are made. They learn to do temporarily without some things because other things—children—offer them greater happiness and satisfaction.

Well, Al, these are my suggestions. It may be a little rough to buckle down to a more rigid financial schedule in the beginning, but you're not too old to learn, and besides, according to the divine plan, Christian parenthood was designed to be a perfecting, developmental experience.

Failure to Accept
Reality Blamed for
Marital Problems

I think my problem is solved—I'm just checking! Looking back over five rough though happy years of marriage, I feel most of my difficulties and disappointments stemmed from failure to accept reality. What a gap between expectations and actual experience! My husband, children, home—all proved so different from what I had dreamed. After five years, I finally see how different, yet how much better, bigger, more significant. Do others learn so slowly, or am I a "queer one"?

∞∞∞∞∞

NO, SUE, you're not queer, but you're maturing; or better, I should say, growing up. All of the really important things in life can be fully understood only through experience. Knowing them from afar or only from the outside is, of course, one form of knowledge, though it tends to be superficial and can be deceptive. Experience, as you have discovered, may prove a rough teacher, ruthlessly brushing aside our world of dreams, unrealistic aspirations, and romantic fancies. Still, we all need her discipline, for she makes us see things as they really are. Paradoxically, our growing up is largely a process of coming down to reality.

I like your observation, Sue, because it applies to all voca-

217

tions. What mature priest is not aware how infinitely more fulfilling has been his life than he dreamed at ordination? What seasoned religious does not look back at her first vow-day and smile at how little she knew about what it means to be a spouse of Christ? And you, like many other brides, have also had to discover that anticipation and experience may be worlds apart.

You say, "reality is so different, yet somehow much better and more significant." I would add, "provided you are willing to learn, to grow up." Yes, there's the rub! Some married people childishly refuse to give up their romantic, premarital fancies. We might say they keep confusing the honeymoon with the whole of marriage, though as a sage remarked, "Marriage begins only after the honeymoon fails." When experience forces them to face reality, they keep saying, "how different," or "if I had only known my partner would be like that," or "if I ever thought that marriage would mean this!"

What has happened to them? Well, Sue, they just quit growing. Somewhere along the line, perhaps at eight or ten, perhaps later, they stopped trying to face life squarely and learned the convenient trick of escaping into their own dreambuilt world. It is not that they lack experience, they simply refuse to learn from it.

In marriage they sometimes pose as frustrated idealists— people with high aims and aspirations who have had the misfortune to be saddled with a dull, insensitive mate. Actually, they are refusing to accept the fact that reality is different from their cherished premarital dream. When I meet them in a counseling situation, I sometimes ask what they really want out of marriage—what changes would they make if they could have their way. Some of them don't know, they just feel frustrated and dissatisfied. Others feel that they know, but as they struggle to put their aims and desires into words, we become aware that they are very much like the small boy who cries when he learns that sand in the sandwiches, flies in the lemonade, and rain at high noon are all part of the picnic.

How happy they could be if they would just come out of their imaginary world and learn to appreciate and enjoy what they have—a faithful partner, children, a job, a home, health, friends, and so forth. Still they persist, "it is all so different, things aren't the way we expected!" Well, if we can't help such people, at least we can profit by their mistakes. Keep learning, keep growing. Our glowing tomorrows will become drab todays only if we expect the noonday light to retain the deceptive romantic tints of sunrise. Reality is different, Sue, but as you say, it can be better and more significant.

Your observation suggests one final thought. If the experience of marriage proves to be so different, yet so much better and fuller than you dreamed, what will the experience of Heaven be like? For "eye hath not seen, nor ear heard, nor hath it entered into the heart of man to know the good things that God hath stored up for those that love Him."

Does Couple
Who Adopts Enjoy
True Parenthood?

After considerable waiting and negotiating, we finally succeeded in adopting our second child a year ago. I guess my wife and I have never been quite so happy, but others don't seem to understand our feelings of joy and pride. They hint we're cackling over somebody else's eggs. Our neighbor even commended us for our charity! We feel we're privileged to be real parents. Are we correct?

～～～～～

EVERY time I see the proud parents of adopted children, I think of those profound, beautiful words of Mary when she and Joseph found their lost Child in the temple: "Thy *Father* and I have sought thee sorrowing." Mary and Jesus called Joseph father. This was no empty title, merely used to cover the mystery of the Virgin Birth, for we read that under Joseph's care, even this Child "advanced in wisdom, and age, and grace with God and men."

Are you real parents? Well, Bob, let's consider carefully what it takes to produce a mature man or woman. To start with, of course, it requires God, the Author of all life, Who creates each immortal soul; and two biological parents, who furnish the co-principles of life. Now if man were a mere creature of instinct, like the animal, all we would have to add

221

to achieve maturity would be the factors of time, nourishment, and, in some species, a degree of early protection.

But man is not a mere creature of instinct. His noblest qualities: supernatural life and the habit of virtuous living, the orderly development of his intellect and will, the learning of self-control, the possession of skills, ideals, and so on, are all acquired after birth. The infant enters life unregenerated and humanly undeveloped, an amazing bundle of potentialties requiring the grace of God and the loving care of others to reach maturity.

Hence his biological parents contribute only his undeveloped nature with its hidden powers. These basic capacities of his being do define, of course, the possibilities or limits of his later physical, emotional, and mental development. Nevertheless, although the human species, taken as a whole, includes individuals with widely varied capacities, the majority of men and women in any given nation are born with roughly the same potentialities. They differ at maturity primarily in the degree to which they have developed what they started out with at birth.

That is why, as Pius XII recently emphasized, the most important aspect of the primary purpose of marriage is education, not procreation. This constitutes the real significance of human parenthood, the truly personal contribution fathers and mothers furnish to the making of a mature man. In transmitting the co-principles of life, they are only, in a sense, acting as middlemen for the human species, since the qualities of the genes they contribute are not primarily the result of their efforts, but come to them from a long line of ancestors.

Yes, Bob, you and your wife share the most important aspect of the privilege of parenthood. Just as the mother's womb forms the essential, nourishing environment in which the tiny life-cell can unfold its marvelous hidden potencies and develop to the stage of independent viability, so your family circle, characterized by loving care, affection, guidance, training, good example and grace, forms the social and spiritual womb requisite for the normal development of children to the stage of independent maturity.

A few weeks ago I was introduced to a mother and her lovely young daughter. When I mentioned how much they resembled each other, she smiled happily and then told me that the daughter was adopted. But the resemblance was there not by chance. Mother and daughter appeared so much alike because example, imitation, and mutual love had been long at work in their family circle.

Bob, when your children reach maturity, the imprint of you and your wife will be found on every facet of their character. Their life-goals, ideals, and capacities for love and affection will necessarily bear your stamp. If this doesn't constitute human parenthood, then what does the term mean?

Vocation of
Single Life Too
Often Disregarded

I am a teacher, unmarried, and probably will remain so. Every year our teenage girls at school listen to retreat conferences on the beauty and dignity of marriage and the religious life, but the single state as a vocation and a possibility that some may have to face or endure is never mentioned. Isn't there some theology of "the single life without vows," which would make it appear less like dull prose? How do we fulfill our role in the Mystical Body?

〰〰〰〰

YOU have raised a long neglected question, Florence. The single woman is a minority in our much-married society so most sermons, retreats, and confessors tend to overlook her special needs. Your letter shows that you recognize the basic dimensions of the problem: Society is geared to the family, and most adult social relationships proceed on the basis of couples. The single woman is consequently under the dual necessity of developing and enriching her personality in some career other than marriage, and she must find legitimate, substitute means for the expression of affection and intimate emotional response. These "compensations" for family life must be significant and enduring enough to satisfy her needs throughout her entire life cycle. Although modern

225

society provides extensive occupational opportunities for the single woman, it offers few substitutes for family life outside of religious communities.

Well, Florence, I see you understand the *social* significance of singlehood. Your problem is: how does your life fit into the divine plan? If God created men and women as complementary helpmates and partners, how do the unmarried achieve fulfillment? Christianity answers that we must keep in mind two aspects of woman's vocation: first, her essential, primary vocation as a human person, requiring growth and development in the knowledge, love, and service of God for its fulfillment; second, her complementary, specifically feminine vocation as a partner to man, implying marriage for total fulfillment. The unmarried woman, whether in a religious community or in the world, achieves the primary purpose of her vocation in life, though she by-passes the complete fulfillment of its specifically feminine aspect of physical motherhood.

Now failure to realize her capacity for motherhood would constitute a serious loss only if this were woman's primary purpose in life, or if it remained a mere negation, implying no fuller development of her other human capacities. Thus, although the dedicated religious by-passes the privilege of motherhood, she fulfills her vocation as a woman by serving God and her fellowmen more perfectly. The singleton in the world must do likewise, though the way she does this is not so clearly defined.

As I see it, Florence, the first requisite for success in your way of life is the full acceptance of what it personally and socially implies. In practice, this means that you will reject the "escapes" sometimes used by others. Don't try to console yourself by pointing out that some married couples are miserable and unhappy in their vocation. There's no reason to feel insecure and to retreat from life as if you had "missed the boat." Don't keep insisting how much freer and happier you are because you never married. Remember, also, that you remain a social being, and since society tends to restrict your associations with men, cultivate and maintain close ties with other girls, your married friends, and the members of your own family.

Avoid the danger of self-centeredness by deepening your understanding of the Mystical Body. To serve Christ in His members, by example and cooperation at work, by the numberless opportunities for sympathy, kindness, and love available in daily contacts with others, by engaging in some of the varied forms of Catholic Action, by rendering witness to Christ through your attitudes and efforts in your career—all these means are at hand provided you see them.

These general directives merely spell out the requisites for all balanced Christian living. More specifically, regard your vocation as a special invitation to sanctity. As St. Paul reminds us, you are freed from many of the consuming concerns of your married sisters and consequently can give yourself more fully to God. Above all, deepen your Christian viewpoint on life. We all tend to look for happiness from without, but true happiness always flows outward from within.

Critical Family
Dampens Girl's Marriage
Prospects

What does a girl do when her family criticizes every young man with whom she goes? I'm already twenty and feel I'm old enough to marry, but my family acts as if none of the boys in our neighborhood are good enough for me. Dad doesn't say much; it's mother and my two brothers who do all the talking. Although I want to follow my parents' advice, how am I ever going to get married at this rate?

<hr/>

YOU know, Betty, your letter puts me on the spot a bit! I have always insisted that parents are obliged to exercise watchfulness and care in helping their children select suitable companions, since friendship leads to love and marriage. Likewise, I have stressed the serious obligation of children to obey their parents and to follow their reasonable advice. When applying these principles to your case, emphasis must be placed on the term *reasonable*.

It is a fact of experience that many parents, and mothers in particular, tend to regard the future mates of their children with a jaundiced eye. I suppose few women feel that another woman could raise someone who would be quite worthy of their own cherished "pride and joy." This is perhaps a necessary consequence of parenthood. All parents nourish glowing hopes for the future of the infants they bear, and long years of loving care frequently contribute little to bring these hopes into focus with reality.

Perhaps an added factor in parental opposition is the unconscious fear of loss. Marriage does take children out of the home and consequently narrows the family circle. Particularly when fathers and mothers have not grown closely together as husbands and wives, they tend to center their interest and affection on their children. The possibility of the child's marriage then appears as a threat to this type of parent-child relationship and will be opposed in various ways. Opposition arising from this cause is all the more difficult to deal with because its source is seldom recognized or admitted. Rather, parents rationalize it as an honest effort to seek the child's best interests.

Under these circumstances, criticism of a possible prospective mate becomes the usual procedure. It is such a subtle, devastating weapon because it gradually destroys respect for the person, whereas true love can be founded and developed only on the basis of mutual respect.

I gather from your letter, Betty, that past criticism has already caused you to drop several young men from your list. You wonder how long this is going to keep up. Well, if the criticism stems from some of the factors I have mentioned, it will continue no matter what kind of man you meet.

What should you do? In the first place, you're old enough to know your own mind and to stand on your own feet. You can't go on picking your friends according to the likes or dislikes of your family. Above all, in selecting your future partner, remember it will be you and not your mother or brothers who will share married life with him.

Second, you know the qualities to look for in a mate. Does he understand and appreciate his faith? Does he have an adequate sense of responsibility, that is, can he hold a job, and is he capable of supporting a family? Is he emotionally balanced and mature, that is, has he grown up yet? Does he respect you and your sense of values? etc., etc.

Third, although common sense tells you to weigh carefully what your parents say, you should not let your judgment of others be swayed by that shallow, carping criticism which belittles everyone outside the family circle. No young man is perfect, but then, neither are you!

What will happen if you do ignore family opposition? Fortunately, Betty, although studies show that a good percentage of future brides or grooms were originally not wholly acceptable to their partner's parents, parental coolness proved temporary in the majority of cases. On the other hand, if it should persist unreasonably, this would be a clear indication that it was unhealthy, and you would have done well to ignore it. Remember, you are looking for your man; it is *your* life and your own happiness that is at stake.

Widow Seeks
Solution to Adjusting
to Life Alone

I'm a widow at forty-six with children nine to seventeen. My husband and I were so close—friends and companions in everything. Never did I dream of what happens when left alone. It's like learning to walk and live again after following a different pattern for twenty-five years. Others must have felt the same. How did they start again? What did they do for their loneliness?

❧❧❧❧❧❧

WHEN death dissolves a happy marriage, the resulting sorrow is truly unique in intensity and nature. Through marriage, husband and wife become "two in one flesh." This special intimacy, based on mutual complementarity and love, necessarily tends over time to fuse and fashion them together through every facet of their being. Death does more than stop this process; it leaves the survivor's life maimed and disjointed. To the pain of loss is added the burden of reorganizing and readjusting the whole complex web of personal relationships. You state it well, Monica, "it's like learning to walk and live again."

Before discussing what to do, let's get some perspective by looking at the overall picture. Approximately one-fourth of all American marriages are in a widowed state at any given time. This means that about one out of every six persons of marriageable age (14 years old and over) is widowed. Owing to the current death rate among men, their greater age at marriage, and the higher remarriage rate of widowers, a little over two-thirds of homes broken by death are fatherless.

How do people react to bereavement? The principal ways are: (1) escape by recourse to drugs, drink, change of residence, social distractions, and suicide; (2) deliberate removal of all reminders both material and mental of the departed one; (3) consolation in religious beliefs or by perpetuating the memory of the deceased; (4) overindulgence in grief or rejection of society and living by oneself; (5) taking over the work of the deceased and carrying on in the same spirit; (6) reattachment of affections to another person or "cause."

As you can see, Monica, some of these ways represent mere escapes or dodges. Others are based on self-pity and personal defeat. Although it may be difficult to define precisely what successful recovery from bereavement would be, it must clearly involve: (1) gradual lessening of the tensions and frustrations resulting from loss: (2) adequate repatterning of love and affectional needs; (3) ability to face obligations and to meet problems related to social life with courage and energy.

You ask how this can be achieved. The answer is simple, though not easy. You must learn to live again as an independent person. For the past twenty-five years you have been living a shared, dependent, mutually supporting, couple existence. Now you must learn to walk alone—just as you did before marriage. Of course your world has changed since then! Today you have memories, children, obligations, acquired habits, and so on, which weigh you down. You feel you are so different now, but are you? As a matter of fact, whether in marriage or out of it, the average person uses only a limited percentage of his actual capacities. It is this reserve which enables us to adapt and adjust to such varied situations—if we have the will to do so.

Where do you start? First, your immediate family circle must be reorganized. Your family must have a head, and that now means you. If special problems of finance, and so forth, arise, seek competent advice—and be willing to learn. Don't say, "these things are beyond me," or, "it's too late to start now!" Likewise, you must rechannel your social life. You are no longer a couple. Many former outlets will be closed. You must discover and maintain adequate substitutes.

What about loneliness? Well, Monica, I don't think you can attack this directly. Although it sounds trite to say so, the degree of loneliness you will experience will depend largely on the amount of time you are alone—not physically alone, but alone with your memories, unoccupied with wider interests, unconcerned with others, uninvolved in absorbing activities. This is not mere escape, it is simply the energetic refusal to live in the past.

Finally, you are not wholly alone. Monica, you know that your husband lives, though separated from you. Under the first shock of loss, it is difficult to grasp this fact. We find it less painful simply not to think, but gradually faith restores the balance. With Martha we can say, "I know that he shall rise again."

What Is Church's
Position on
"Over-Population" Issue

Lately, I've been receiving considerable literature on the problem of over-population. The last piece to arrive at the office speaks of the "population bombshell" and carries frightening quotations from a long list of important people. It says the Church's stand is the big obstacle to reasonable action, citing one Protestant theologian as saying Roman Catholics had better revise their views. Are we ignoring the problem? What is the Catholic position?

※※※※※※

NO, ED, the Church isn't ignoring the problem. Pius XII has dealt with it time and again in the last twenty years. I know the literature you mention. Unfortunately, the "important people" frequently cited have little training in population problems. They are frightened by the expansion of Communism among the economically under-developed countries and see one easy method of raising the standard of living: cut the birth rate. Some of the current "scare" literature goes further, stating the world, and even America, is rapidly running out of resources.

What do the trained population experts tell us? First, they do not speak of the population *problem*, but of problems. The situation and its solution differ from country to country.

Second, they do not define these problems as simple ratios between people and resources. Owing to modern advances, our resources may be regarded as practically unlimited. The crux of the problem is shortage of capital, organization, and "know how" to exploit them in many countries.

Third, although adequate, usable, and reliable statistics are sadly lacking for many major regions, it seems clear that world population is expanding rapidly at present. This growth is closely related to recent advances in health care and its greater availability.

Fourth, they insist we cannot yet predict future growth trends. They reject the simple projection of present trends into the future, as is commonly done in popular literature to create a frightening picture. We have not discovered any universally applicable "laws" of population growth.

Fifth, they emphasize the present lack of adequate data and theory. As population expert Philip Hauser, of the University of Chicago, told the World Population Conference held in Rome in 1954, "We are particularly ill-equipped to provide policy makers and administrators with an adequate factual basis for social engineering purposes."

Well, Ed, this is the way the trained experts view the situation. Population problems are serious in many regions, proposed solutions must be tentative and varied, though most imply some reduction in present growth trends. I can't discuss these solutions here, but I did want you to get the facts straight.

What is the Church's position? First, to correct a common misunderstanding, the Catholic ideal does not emphasize mere numbers or family size. Children are one of the great blessings of marriage, but their ideal number is relative to the capacities of the individual couple who must procreate and rear them to maturity.

Second, the Church is deeply concerned about the methods used to limit population size. She condemns abortion as murder, the use of any of the varied forms of contraceptives (birth control) as sinful, and direct sterilization as a form of unlawful mutilation. Further, she teaches that marriage partners may choose to refrain from marital relations either absolutely or periodically in order to control family size, provided they both agree to this, they are capable, and they have sufficient reason. Finally, the popes have constantly insisted on a better distribution of wealth, and the need for advanced nations to assist those in need.

Ed, you well know that it is not the function of the Church to advance any detailed plans for dealing with over-population. Catholic teaching defines the moral dimensions or framework of the problem, and it is up to population experts and other scientists to work out solutions on the basis of these terms. The Church does not ignore the problem, but she insists it cannot be solved by methods which destroy human dignity and frustrate man's purpose in life.

The Church has always insisted on control, but control of the sexual drive, not control (destruction) of its reproductive consequences. She teaches that population problems can be solved if men use science for production rather than destruction. But this implies the very self-control which most modern programs openly reject. In this connection, the great Indian leader, Gandhi, remarked, "It was reserved for our generation to glorify vice by calling it virtue."

What Is Needed to
Make Intelligent Decision
on Religious Vocation

When is a girl old enough to make up her own mind about what she will be in life? I've wanted to enter the religious life since I was in sixth grade. Because I'm an only child, my parents are very much opposed and are even sending me to a public high school so I won't be "prompted" by priests or sisters. I don't want to disobey my parents, but I'm sixteen now and feel I'm old enough to make my own decisions. What do you think?

❧❧❧❧❧❧

WELL, Agnes, there are decisions and decisions. We're old enough to make our own decisions when we're old enough to know the necessary facts, the pertinent principles, and how to apply these logically to the case under discussion. This isn't really a function of age, but of knowledge and prudent judgment. In making decisions which have far-reaching consequences, such as choosing our life vocation, we must proceed slowly and with care.

You tell me that you have been praying a lot and reading books on the religious life for the past six years. Such perseverance in spite of no outside support from parents or teachers is a good sign you're not daydreaming or letting your

241

imagination run away with you. Aren't you now old enough to make up your own mind in regard to your vocation?

We can probably answer that question better if we see what is needed to make an intelligent decision in this matter. First, what qualities are required for success in a vocation to the religious life? Stated briefly, you must have the intention of consecrating yourself to the service of God and the salvation of souls, together with the necessary physical, intellectual and moral endowments. You apparently have the right intention, enjoy good health, are doing well in your studies, and are obedient and persevering.

Second, since you are not going to start your own order —I hope—you have to select some religious congregation engaged in the type of work you feel you would be able to do, and in which you would like to serve God. Is it nursing? Teaching? Missionary work? Contemplation? There are religious congregations established for almost every variety of work, and many of them combine several major types.

Third, because you have been reading about the religious life, I take it for granted that you have a general idea concerning the vows, rules, and way of life which religious congregations uniformly observe.

Fourth, although you owe respect and obedience to your parents, they have taken such an unchristian attitude toward your vocation that one may well question their judgment in this matter. At any rate, it is impossible to justify their decision to transfer you to a public school so that you would not be encouraged in your vocation by priests or sisters. Since you tell me, "they don't want me to enter now or later," I think we can safely assume that their judgment in this matter is not based on sound moral principles and can consequently be ignored.

What should you do? Well, Agnes, if you think you have the proper qualifications, if you know enough about the religious life to understand what such a vocation implies, and if you have prayed over the matter as you indicate, I think you are "old enough" to make your own decision in this regard.

Your next step will be to consult a spiritual director, your confessor or any priest you feel you can talk to with confidence. Explain your views and put yourself under his direction. If he feels that you have a vocation, he can then help you select some religious community for further study. When you enter will depend upon your mutual decision, and, of course, the permission of the religious superiors.

What about your parents? Since you are only sixteen, you may have a problem trying to enter at once, as you now desire. On the other hand, it is possible that your spiritual director can talk to them and help modify their erroneous views. Some parents have acquired strange prejudices against sisters and convents. They object that they do not want to "lose" their daughter by giving her to Christ. This is a strange perversion of Christian thinking. Oddly enough, these same parents do not hesitate to "lose" their daughter in marriage, even though she may move far away from them under present conditions of mobility.

Some Christians evidently think very little of Our Lord, the Divine Spouse.

Husband's Reading Habits
Encompass Only
Sports and Westerns

How can I change my husband's reading habits? Outside the sports page, he reads mostly pocket-size westerns and mysteries. Lately, our two boys still in grade school are trying to imitate him, though I don't think they get much out of the stories. It would be too bad if they formed the habit, but I'm afraid they will if he continues. How can I get him to read some good Catholic literature?

❧❧❧❧❧

I THINK it was Bacon who said, "Reading maketh a full mind." Your question, Laura, is full of—what? If one reads trash, that's what one will carry in his mind. Not that all westerns and mysteries are trash, but a solid diet of them is rather cheap intellectual pabulum. Besides, judging from their covers, the majority appear to be little more than thinly disguised means for discussing sex and brutality. Of course, you have some grounds for rejoicing, your husband has apparently graduated from the large class of adult comic book readers!

In all seriousness, Laura, you do face a real problem. Adults who subsist on such literary fare are either escapists— they want to avoid the effort of thinking, or morons—they are incapable of much thinking. I rather think the majority are escapists. They avoid reading anything solid or spiritual because this would disturb the even tempo of their more or less biological existence. They live in a small, habit-controlled world in which their interests seldom extend beyond their job, food, sex, sports, and recreation. When all goes well, one day in their lives is pretty much like the last, while the sports page furnishes them with an inexhaustible subject of conversation, and their reading of paper-backs, a little safe, vicarious experience in the crudely fascinating world of brutality, sex and murder.

Have I painted an exaggerated picture? Watch their actions, listen to the habitual run of their conversation, ask their opinion on any subject outside their narrow world of interests. Even with increased leisure, we find no widening of mental horizons, only more of the same.

How can you effect a change? Well, Laura, I think you have to approach the task indirectly. Attempts at direct persuasion won't get you very far, but there are other ways available.

First, see to it that there is good literature around the home. This should include some well selected periodicals and books, both Catholic and secular. It is amazing how empty many homes are of such literature. People who do not hesitate to spend freely on entertainment or travel often display a strange reluctance to buy a book or purchase a subscription to a good magazine. How many Americans have ever ventured inside a bookstore? How many ever enter a library after they leave school?

Second, plan your attack on your husband's reading habits. Ask him to read an article or a paragraph you feel is particularly interesting. Get his opinion on it, discuss it with him—he may rise to the occasion once his masculine pride is aroused. This is more than mutual education, it is an enduring bond of unity.

Third, provide appropriate reading material for your children. Pick out passages you feel they will like and have them read these to you or vice versa. Take them to the appropriate departments in the library and let them select their own books. When they are older, you can frequently get them to read an article or even a book if you and your husband discuss parts of it when they're around. Young people like to be in on the conversation, even at the cost of having to read something.

Finally, your best overall approach in this, as in so many other areas, will be your own example. By insisting that good literature be available around the home and by reading it yourself, you will best show your esteem for it. This will impress your children more than anything you may tell them— they learn primarily by imitating those they love.

What about your husband? He's not immune to your example, and if good reading material is available, his curiosity may eventually get the best of him. Remember, Laura, there's some hope for him—he's not reading comic books.

How Much Time Do
Mothers Have for Work
in Parish Affairs?

How active in parish affairs should the parents, particularly the mother of a large family be? In our parish there is some resentment because mothers with four, five, or more small children can't do too much in the Altar Society, Scouts, etc. I get tired of hearing women with only one, or two, or no small children constantly praised for their activity. Why is there so little understanding of big families, especially when the children are small?

≈≈≈≈≈≈

YOU'RE not the first to raise these questions, Ann. Many mothers with a house full of small children feel that they receive little recognition for the important work they are doing. Attention and praise go to those who are active outside the home. This is something of a paradox for Catholics who place such high esteem upon motherhood and family life. Perhaps if we examine the parish setting more closely we can see how this situation may arise.

First, every active parish requires a series of societies, organizations, and committees for its smooth operation. All members of the parish have an obligation to cooperate in this work according to their respective capacities. Second, as in all such voluntary activities, some members cooperate generously and faithfully, while others sit back and let "Joe" do it. Third, it is not surprising that those who are interested in securing cooperation should go out of their way to praise the active members. Fourth, and this is the all too human element in the picture, it is easy to forget that these are not the most important activities in the parish, that mothers with small children, engaged in a much more important work, may simply not have time to cooperate fully in other parish activities. These mothers may not be sitting back to let "Josie" do it, they may have more pressing demands upon their time and energy.

You ask, Ann, why there is so little sympathy and understanding for big families, especially during the years when the children are small. One reason is mere thoughtlessness— people don't stop to reflect on the normal, routine problems a big family necessarily presents. To be sure, mothers who have cars and can afford baby-sitters may have somewhat more time for parish affairs, but they tend to be the exception in the average parish.

The second cause stems from an unrecognized element of secularism in the minds of some Catholics. Although they profess to agree with the Church that numerous children are a blessing, this is one blessing they are quite happy to forego. In reality, they don't appreciate or respect a large family and consequently can't sympathize with its problems.

Now, Ann, let's return to your first question. How active in parish affairs should mothers of large families be? I think I've indicated all the principles needed to formulate an adequate answer. First, there is a hierarchy of values in parish activities. A mother's first obligation is to her home and children. Second, it follows that in being a good mother, you are making the best contribution you can make to the parish.

Third, if you are fortunate enough to have some time and energy to spare, join with others in promoting parish activities. Just remember that for the present, your best contribution *to the parish* will be made in your home.

What will happen to parish activities if all mothers take this view? Well, I answer in the first place, if parish affairs are now taking mothers away from their most important work in the home, they are doing more harm to the parish than good. Second, mothers with small children constitute only a limited percentage of parishioners. Their essential work is clearly cut out for them while their children are small. Later, they will have leisure and energy to make a larger contribution.

In this connection I would like to point out the peculiar distribution of work in the modern mother's life. She tends to be almost too busy during the childbearing and child rearing stage, and too idle once this is accomplished. The average lifespan of American women is steadily increasing, indeed, as one cynic has remarked, "Once they reach the age of forty, modern women become almost indestructible!" Hence mothers have many years in which to make their contribution to parish affairs. Wouldn't a better distribution of labor make more sense?

I suppose, Ann, there will always be some thoughtlessness in the way we regard faithful workers. But your happiness as a mother is not based on public esteem—your children remain your enduring blessing.

I'm Irish;
He's Italian; and
Mother Is Upset

I'm nineteen and have been going with Joe for about two months. Mother is making my life very unhappy. She leaves the room when he comes and insists she'll never speak to me again if I marry him. You see, Joe is Italian and I'm Irish, and that's what upsets mother most. Father likes him and I've found his parents to be wonderful, friendly people. Joe is beginning to mean a great deal to me, but I don't want to hurt mother. What can I do?

❧❧❧❧❧❧

YOUR letter interests me, Rita, because it shows that national differences are still recognized and keenly felt by some people. Most Americans tend to deny this. They feel it is undemocratic, but we can't alter facts by denying they exist. Unfortunately, differences tend to be regarded as marks of inferiority. As the little Mexican boy in California explained when asked to define a minority, "It's people who are considered different—and worse."

Just what national group tends to be at the bottom of the social totem pole varies from region to region and from time to time. Whenever people of different national backgrounds start living together in the same region, a type of social prestige system usually develops, according to which some

253

groups are ranked higher than others. The original basis for this ranking may be wealth, education, religion, power, language, or mere numbers.

Experience also shows that the ranking persists long after its basis in fact ceases to exist. In other words, a group image, a national stereotype, tends to be created in people's minds: All Germans, or Poles, or Italians, or Irish, etc., are ambitious, or lazy, or slow, or intelligent, etc. Strangely enough, even when they know several members of a national group who clearly contradict the false image, most people tend to regard them as exceptions to the rule and never question the soundness of their opinion concerning the national group in general.

This tendency of preconceived images or stereotypes to persist unchallenged in our minds is also at the root of most racial prejudice. When we meet a member of another race, we tend to interpret his words and actions in terms of our national image, rather than to check the validity of this image against our new experience.

Well, Rita, I'm not going to read you a lesson on group prejudices, but I think it will help you deal with your problem if you understand something of its origin. On the other hand, we must not ignore the facts. National differences do exist, and some of them persist for generations even in our conformist society. Particularly in family matters, national traits concerning food, the raising of children, the influence and closeness of relatives, and so forth, are frequently retained and, in many cases, adopted by outsiders.

Now the first pertinent question in your case, Rita, is whether the possible existence of national differences, either your own or Joe's, will hinder success in marriage. You can answer this by finding out whether you agree on the nature and purpose of marriage, the statuses and roles of husband

and wife in the family, and so on. If you want success in marriage, you will have to answer this question satisfactorily, no matter whom you marry, even, as you say "an Irish guy" of your mother's own choosing.

Second, what about the loss of social prestige if you marry Joe? This seems to bother your mother. I think you will find that the present generation of young Americans pays little attention to this as long as you are successful. Your mother evidently was raised in a different climate of opinion and finds it difficult to change.

You ask, Rita, what can I do to avoid hurting Mother? Well, in the first place, your father is on your side. Although most men are no match for their wives in such matters, he can probably help you modify her opinion. At the same time, you have the assurance that he likes Joe, so you may feel greater confidence in your own attitude.

Finally, this is your marriage. You don't want to hurt your mother, but her attitude is unreasonable and consequently cannot serve as a guide. If you cannot change her attitude at present, you should ignore it prudently and respectfully. Sooner or later, every maturing person must learn to stand up for what he thinks is right, even though those who are dear to him feel otherwise. This occurs frequently in choosing a religious vocation; it may occur in choosing a marriage partner. You and your mother may as well start learning that lesson right now.

Proper Attitudes Important
in Answering
Child's Question

What should you tell your seven-year-old daughter when she asks why "mommy's tummy" is getting big? I'm carrying our sixth and it's becoming noticeable. We know she has talked with the neighbor's children about other women in my condition. We want to do what's right, but don't know how much to tell or how to tell it.

❧❧❧❧❧❧❧

ACCORDING to experts, Nina, little girls, like their mothers, notice everything! As you say, she has already discussed the subject of pregnancy with her friends and has undoubtedly received considerable information or misinformation by now. This means that you are starting your instructions a little late. I don't think there's much cause for worry, however, because your little daughter apparently feels free to ask you questions. As long as she keeps coming to you for the right answers, you have no reason to feel concern.

But you want to know when, how much, and how to tell her the things that she ought to know. Since you have other children who must be instructed, and many other couples have raised these same questions, let's start out by stating a few broad principles covering this area of parental instruction.

First, in the child's early years, parents are regarded as

the chief source of knowledge. The child thinks of them as people who have all the answers. If they don't answer his routine questions concerning sex, his curiosity will be aroused and he'll seek information elsewhere.

Second, don't project your adult feelings and attitudes into the child's questions. During the early years, the child asks innumerable, random, superficial questions about everything. If his curiosity isn't specially alerted by your reaction to his questions, he doesn't stay at any one subject very long. Hence, questions should be answered truthfully, but in the broad, superficial way they are asked. As someone has remarked, you can tell your children are growing up when they start asking questions that really make sense.

Third, your little girl is old enough to start asking questions that make sense, and she had best get the answers from you. Remember, sex is not yet a personal matter to her. She wants information, both because her mind is made to know, and she doesn't like to appear dumb to her little playmates. Tell her simply, in your own words, that God has blessed you, and you are carrying a baby. What details you give her will depend upon how much she already knows. She'll probably come back to the subject frequently, and you can extend her knowledge as you see fit. Proper attitudes rather than detailed facts are important: joy, wonder, and gratitude at the way that God and her parents are cooperating in the "miracle" of producing a new baby sister or brother.

Fourth, boys and girls develop differently, ask different questions, and tend to have different needs for instruction in this as in all other matters. You will learn this from the different questions they ask.

Fifth, there are two broad, closely related but distinct stages in acquiring mature attitudes toward sex. During the first stage, emphasis is on facts, not feelings. The whole matter is impersonal. At puberty, however, sex is recognized as an intimately personal quality. Curiosity and the desire for information are still operative, but since sex now becomes a highly personal affair, parents should take it for granted that the adolescent also needs the counsel of a spiritual director.

I recognize, Nina, that many parents like yourself seek more than general directives. An excellent book designed for your needs has been written by Father Henry Sattler: *Parents, Children, and the Facts of Life* (St. Anthony Guild Press, Paterson, N. J. It also appears in a popular, paper-back edition). This work discusses the what, how, and the when in a way that all parents can understand.

Although parents should be concerned about the instruction and guidance of their children in this matter, there is no cause for undue anxiety. Rely on your common sense, the sacramental grace of your parental vocation, and prayer. You are not alone in raising your children. They are also God's "little ones," to whom He gives graces according to their needs.

My Wife Resents
My "Night Out
with the Boys"

*My wife raises a great fuss every time I want a night out
with the boys. She says she just can't see what I get out
of playing cards in a smoky room and drinking beer for
hours, while she sits home with the kids. Women enjoy
their parties, too, though they generally have them in the
afternoon when we're not at home anyway. Am I being
thoughtless and selfish in wanting to get out once in a
while? She thinks so.*

~~~~~~~~

ACCORDING to the comic strips, Ted, this marital argument has been going on for a long time and isn't likely
to stop. Perhaps it is more acute now that the husband's job
separates the majority of couples all during the day, so that
they spend such little time together. We might guess that a
less highly industrialized society, which permits husbands and
wives to be closer together during the working day, would
also find them more willing to seek separate entertainment
at night. That's probably why parish societies in the past
were organized according to sex, whereas today only the
couple-centered movements tend to be accepted.

At any rate, Ted, you have a problem, and it's evidently
not being solved to anybody's satisfaction. You don't want to

be unfair, yet you think your wife is being a little narrow and inconsiderate. She would probably say the same about you, so arguing about it doesn't help matters very much.

What's the solution, if any? It will help clarify matters if you both start out by recognizing that there are no absolute principles or norms which clearly specify what is right and wrong in such situations. Social customs, conditions, and individual couples differ so greatly that satisfactory solutions vary widely. In a sense, your problem is unique. It can be worked out only in terms of your total marriage situation.

This doesn't mean that a good solution will be wholly arbitrary. There are guiding norms and pertinent considerations which should shape your thinking if you sincerely want to reach an agreement that will strengthen your marriage. Let's go over the principal ones briefly.

First, marriage does imply companionship and partnership as a couple. This involves not only cooperation in childbearing and child rearing but intimate, affectionate unity, for only if husband and wife are thus closely united can they maintain the loving, emotionally secure family climate which children need for normal development.

Second, because of personality differences and previous training, men and women in marriage frequently discover that they do not share each other's likes or dislikes. This may have little to do with their love or unity, but since they now form a couple, it limits the things they can share and may lead to misunderstanding. Some people regard all differences as marks of inferiority. If you don't like what they like, you must have poor taste!

Third, particularly during the early child rearing stages, the wife's social life may be seriously restricted. After spending the day with immature children, she craves adult companionship. Husbands easily tend to forget this.

Fourth, all marriages require a degree of give and take. This defies close calculation. The important point is to preserve the spirit of mutual service and support. Once bickering and bargaining start, marriage becomes a type of "cold war."

How should you solve your problem, Ted? First, make a check of the number of times you take your wife out at night. If you can't afford it or simply neglect it, are you surprised she resents your night with the boys? Second, how often do you want to go out alone? Surely more than once a week would indicate a peculiar attitude toward your wife and family. Indeed, this would be too often if you didn't take her out an equal number of times. You say, "this would be too expensive," or "she doesn't want to leave the children that often?" Then you had best reconsider your own request.

Fourth, if your wife's only objection to your night out is that she doesn't approve of what you do, I think she's probably making a mistake. She should recall the old Roman saying, "One can't argue about tastes."

Finally, in solving your problem, take a long range view of your marriage. It is for life. What you do now will shape its future course for better or worse. Remember, in love as in war, you may win a battle but lose the campaign.

Parents-in-Law Are
Trying to
Run Our Lives

How can I get my husband's parents to see that we want to lead a life of our own? He's an only child, and in the fourteen months we've been married, they have been over here most of the time they're not working. I like them, but they tend to take over. I've finally managed to get her out of the kitchen, now my problem is to keep her from trying to raise our baby. Our home is the only place they visit, so when they have nothing to do, they drive over here. What can I do?

☧☧☧☧

WELL, Janice, your problem is an old one, though you seem to have it in a rather acute form. It points up the fact that "weaning" is a two-way process. It's the same whether in infancy or later life, both parent and child must accept what it implies and repattern their lives accordingly. Your husband's parents haven't grasped the full implications of his marriage. This may be a little difficult for them because he is their only child.

Your problem is further complicated by the fact that they enjoy such a narrow social life. This seems rather unusual in a modern urban setting, though, as you mention in your letter, they both hold full-time jobs, so this may provide some explanation.

How can you handle this situation, Janice? Let's review some of the pertinent aspects of the problem before planning a solution. First, I'm happy to note that you like your husband's parents. They apparently like you, too, and that's the way it should be.

Second, it's clear that their intentions are all right. They may be thoughtless and perhaps, even inconsiderate under the circumstances, but there's no indication of ill will.

Third, family patterns differ a great deal. Among some, parents and married children are very close, even to the extent of living in the same house or next door to each other. This was rather common among some national groups, although modern living conditions tend to modify it among their second and third generation descendants. In itself, this arrangement is neither good nor bad, it depends primarily on local customs and the way people are trained.

Fourth, most young wives and mothers tend to feel somewhat insecure in their new roles and consequently are highly sensitive to outside interference. This is quite understandable. In their first ventures at cooking and housekeeping, they are eager to prove to themselves and to others that they are capable of doing a good job, while the care of their first baby is both a challenge and a source of concern unparalleled in their previous experience.

These are some of the possible factors in your problem, Janice. Now, what should you do? First, analyze your own attitudes. Are you perhaps a little over-sensitive? Is the situation really a serious threat to your happiness, or is it an irritation you resent but can manage to live with?

Second, talk it over with your husband. Explain how you

feel about the situation, and get him to cooperate with you in working out some plan for dealing with it. Don't tackle it singlehanded. This is his problem as much as yours, for your marital happiness may be involved. Although most men are rather helpless under such circumstances, if you learn to think and plan together, no outside interference can disrupt your union.

Third, you may have to proceed slowly—weaning is a gradual process! Start out by building up your social life on your own as a couple. Make plans to go out together, to associate with other couples, and so forth. In this way you will keep your family life from being dominated by his parents. They may be upset or disappointed at first, but this is part of their weaning process.

Finally, don't blow your top or do anything you may later regret. Remember, Janice, they like you and they mean well. You may have to be firm on occasion, but keep your emotions in check. Try to take a long range view of the process. After all, you've already made some progress—you've got her out of the kitchen.

How Can You Tell
When You're
Really in Love?

How do you know when you're really in love? Jerry and I have been engaged for some time, but it will be almost a year before we can marry because we want to finish school. Experience has taught us to avoid certain displays of affection, and we attend Mass together every morning. Lately, however, I find myself noticing many little faults in Jerry. These seem to irritate me a good deal, so I'm seriously wondering whether I'm really in love. I know he loves me. How can I be sure I love him?

~~~~~~~

TO TELL the truth, Marge, one can never be absolutely sure of human love. Since it consists in the union of wills, it is essentially a spiritual thing. You can't see it or weigh it. Human love must always be taken on faith. But human faith always leaves a little room for uncertainty. I suppose that's why people in love keep saying so over and over again. That's why lovers feel the need to back up their words with repeated gestures of affection, signifying their unity and dedication.

Though you can't be absolutely sure, Marge, there are ways of reaching a reasonably prudent judgment in the matter. In the first place, remember that the type of love you really want is domestic love. By this I mean that you are not concerned with forming some kind of vague man-woman companionship with Jerry. You are planning to build a life-companionship in marriage, implying intimate partnership in childbearing and child rearing.

Hence your first question should be, does he have the requisite traits and attitudes for such companionship? Remember, Marge, you can love someone, or think you love him, though you could never build a successful marriage with him. Men and women do this every day in our society, and because they forget that successful marriage requires domestic love and the qualities that go with it, they enter marriage in "love," and the divorce court in disgust.

Paradoxically, some of the poorest marriage prospects in our society are apparently quite loveable characters. Entertaining, irresponsible, undisciplined play boys—and play girls—may be highly popular and attractive; they are no candidates for successful marriage. Likewise, emotionally immature and overly dependent men strongly attract some girls. Perhaps this is their "mothering instinct," but whatever it is, they had best save it for their children.

What traits should you look for in Jerry? Well, Marge, since he attends mass with you each morning, he apparently values his faith. He's going to get his degree next year, so he'll probably be able to support you and the children. Is he emotionally balanced? Reasonably mature for his age? From roughly the same family background, so that your manners, attitudes, and family aspirations do not clash too greatly?

I rather think, Marge, that the above is not your problem. You are wondering about the "little things" that now seem to irritate you for the first time. Are they serious? Let's look at the situation a little more closely. You have been engaged for some time, yet you are not now preoccupied with immediate plans for your marriage. In a sense, this is an abnormal gap. You are two adults in love, but circumstances beyond your control force you from moving towards the normal culmination of that love in marriage. Now courtship love may be emotionally loaded; it remains nevertheless a relatively shallow love, lacking the solid underpinnings of the shared experience and deep personal intimacy found in domestic love. It is very likely that your prolonged engagement is revealing little faults which domestic love would discover but consider of little importance.

Furthermore, Marge, whether you recognize it or not, your prolonged engagement places both of you under an emotional strain. You mention that you have learned to avoid certain displays of affection. You are correct in doing so, and though you consciously accept this restraint for moral reasons, it is difficult not to harbor some unconscious resentment that you cannot follow your normal impulses to show affection. Under these circumstances, your feelings toward each other may be divided (ambivalent). You love each other, yet the object of your love is also a source of frustration. It is not surprising that this may escape as faultfinding or irritation at times.

What should you do? I feel that once you recognize the likely source of your problem, you will be able to solve it. No, Marge, you can never be absolutely sure of being in love; though in your case, I'd give mighty big odds that you are.

Why Are Parents Being
Blamed for
Juvenile Delinquency?

What's so wrong with the modern parents? We knock ourselves out to feed, clothe and shelter our children, we send them to school, we give them more freedom, spending money, and leisure than we ever enjoyed, yet every time we pick up the paper, we read about some "expert" who says we're making a mess of it. I know there's a terrific juvenile delinquency problem, but if it's our fault, why don't they tell us what we're doing wrong?

※※※※※※

THAT'S a good question, Jerry. Unfortunately, few of the experts seem to agree on what's wrong, so they're not likely to agree on solutions. Just to keep the record straight, it should be noted that a large block of modern parents are doing a good job. Their children aren't delinquents; in fact, they don't even belong to that peculiar modern category called "teenagers." They're just normal kids, passing through the usual stages of development leading to maturity.

As you realize, of course, changed social conditions offer new problems for both parents and children. Let's review these briefly before considering what parents can do about them.

From the viewpoint of parents, many new influences such

as radio, television, cars, and so forth, affect young people today and increase parental problems. Likewise, the family has less social importance today, so that young people tend to spend more time with their peer group, the gang. At the same time, the father's job tends to take him away from the home much of the time, with the result that mother has to take over the rearing of children and father's influence in the family circle becomes minimal.

From the viewpoint of young people, modern society places undue stress on irresponsibility, lack of seriousness, and having a good time during youth. Likewise, it places many young people in a social vacuum—they don't want to go to school, yet they are too young to be employed. Finally, although boys and girls reach biological maturity well in advance of the age at which it is customary to marry in our society, their prolonged, intimate, relatively unsupervised association is widely tolerated, if not openly promoted. They are given little instruction and protection, while the exploitation of the sexual drive is freely permitted in advertising, literature, and entertainment.

What can parents do under these conditions? Their essential task remains the same. As always, they must guide, teach, and support their growing children in the difficult process which goes on within youth as they strive to reach the balance of maturity. Children must learn the norms, moral rules, and modes of conduct expected by their parents and society. As their powers and faculties develop, they must acquire the habit of controlling and directing their impulses and drives according to approved standards. In this process, parents are present not only to teach and encourage, more important, they serve as models. Children learn by imitation.

Hence, it is not sufficient to feed, clothe, and protect your children. You must give them ideals, something to strive for in life as men and women. What is the meaning of life? What are the goals worth working for? What qualities of character, what formal training do they require? You must put something "inside" your children. This gradual task of character formation, of "building in" motives, self-discipline, life-goals and aspirations is the most important job that parents have.

Don't think you are being good to your children by protecting them from hard work in school, a sense of responsibility, and the "harsh" realities of life. Youth likes a challenge. Young people should not be protected as little children. They are quite capable of responsibility and serious thought, for they are young men and women well on the way toward maturity. Help them develop worthwhile life-goals. Show them that what they now do in school will pretty well decide what they will be later in life. They have energy, strength, and endurance to spare; if it is unmotivated and undirected, we shouldn't be surprised if they use it destructively.

So, Jerry, don't stew over the criticism of the experts. Do your job, as your father did before you, and your children will be your reward.

Husband's Criticism of
Wife Becomes
Unreasonable

Shouldn't a man show respect for his wife? My husband criticizes me in front of our children and even in the presence of outsiders. He never misses a chance to pick me up on a mistake, so that sometimes I think he's just waiting for me to pull a boner. Lately, he's been making disparaging remarks about my family. When I protest, he pretends he's only teasing. What makes a man act that way?

~~~~~~~

I'M NOT sure Louise; maybe he's developed an ulcer! In all seriousness, though, you do face a distressing problem. Your letter suggests that his critical attitude is something new or, at least, has taken a turn for the worse at present. This may provide a clue to its origin, though with my present knowledge of the problem, I can only suggest several possibilities.

As you know from experience, loss of respect in marriage causes real suffering when it is manifested in critical remarks and obvious attempts to humiliate the partner. More significant, it may indicate a loss of love. True love is always founded on mutual respect. When respect is lacking, there may remain emotional, sensual, or sexual attraction, but not love, and such relationship usually indicates exploitation. The reason is that true love involves a relationship between persons, and the human person demands respect because it is the highest value in creation. If so-called lovers do not respect each other, this shows that they regard each other as objects or things, hence the likelihood of exploitation.

Lest this bit of philosophy eludes you, Louise, just remember that there is no true love without respect; and conversely, where there is no respect, there can be no true love. If young men and women remembered this on dates, they would be less likely to mistake affectionate exploitation for true love. When "lover-boy" says or implies, "If you really loved me, you would do this," he's not talking about true love!

Now to your problem, Louise. What makes a man act that way? Let's survey some of the possibilities. First, have you made him feel that you're competing with him? Sometimes husbands think that their wives are trying to outshine them and use this indirect way to cut them down to size. Wives may do this unconsciously, and if their husbands are insecure, they may react in this immature fashion.

Second, are you at odds with your husband in some other area of marital or family relationships? Again, this may be your husband's indirect way of showing resentment over an unwilling concession or defeat in some other area. This is typical strategy in marital disagreements.

Third, is your tongue sharper and more critical than you realize? Some people lack empathy—the ability to put themselves in the other fellow's shoes so as to see how he thinks and feels. Hence they may remain quite unconscious of how their words and actions affect others, though they are highly sensitive to what is done to themselves. We all know people who "can't take a joke," yet delight in pulling them on others.

Fourth, maybe you're just growing up, that is, assuming a mature role in marriage after posing as a more or less flighty, care-free school girl, and your husband can't adjust to the change. Some girls pose as mental lightweights during courtship and early marriage because this seems to flatter a certain type of husband. When they start acting maturely, their husbands may resent it as a threat to their masculine superiority.

These are some of the possibilities, Louise. Look them over carefully for any light they may throw on your problem. What else can you do?

You will be on safe ground if you try to bolster up your husband's self-confidence and sense of security as head of the family. Don't hesitate to compliment and praise whenever possible. This should be mutual among normal couples, of course, but you will be wise to start it yourself.

More directly, if your husband stubbornly persists, you had best have a showdown. Don't let him pass his criticism off as mere teasing. Ask him why he feels so insecure, what score he's trying to even up, what he hopes to gain by hurting you. These questions may open his eyes.

Above all, don't let his criticism undermine your own sense of security and self-confidence. As wife and mother, you're queen of the home. Act the part, and your children, at least, will never doubt it.

How Long Must I
Help Pay
My Sister's Bills?

When my good parents died eight years ago, my single sister kept the home and was partially supported by our alcoholic brother. Since then she has done nothing to help herself financially, and when my married sister and I spoke to her of employment, she became quite annoyed. Now she is in her late forties, though she doesn't look it, and depends almost entirely upon us. I don't want to be uncharitable, but must I go on helping her if she refuses to help herself?

〜〜〜〜〜〜

IF I UNDERSTAND your family situation correctly, Grace, your single sister has never been employed outside the home. As you state in another part of your letter, you married late because you had to help support the parental home for many years. This may complicate your problem somewhat. Your single sister has remained at home, and since you have continued to take responsibility for the financial difficulties of both her and your brother, she has developed a long pattern of dependency in this regard.

How much longer must you continue to pick up her bills? Well, Grace, I think you have been doing it much too long already. Before offering some suggestions for dealing with the problem, let's review a few pertinent principles.

First, we can all agree that charity should begin at home. Family members are bound together by strong, enduring bonds of nature and affection. They should mutually help each other according to their various needs and capacities.

Second, true charity is based on justice, though it extends beyond it. In the present case, justice demands that your sister make a sincere effort to help herself. As a mature woman in good health, she has no right to be dependent on the efforts of others for her financial support. As the apostle put it, "If he will not work, neither let him eat."

Third, true charity looks to the total good of the person. Your sister is harming herself by refusing to make some effort to become financially independent. The older she gets, the more insecure and dependent she will become. The Creator did not make us parasites, and we are bound to lose our dignity and self-respect if we try to be such. Whether your sister's attitude is motivated by sloth, or fear of venturing outside the home, it is spiritually and psychologically unhealthy. Hence you will fail in charity if you allow her to continue in this state.

How can you go about getting her to take a more realistic view of the situation? First, I think you and your married sister should come to an agreement that you are going to take a definite stand in dealing with her. Second, you had best set her down and tell her the facts of life. Don't be upset if she becomes annoyed at the suggestion that she make some sincere effort to help herself. She's old enough to know she has no right to expect you to go on supporting her, and not too old to learn to do something for herself. Indeed, it would be well to point out that she has a good many years of life ahead of her. At present, she's starting to retire into her shell and die pretty young.

Third, you and your sister should make every effort to find employment suitable to her taste and talents. If she needs some additional training to get started, encourage her and help her out. This will be true Christian charity since you will be helping her to help herself, rather than reducing her to the status of a parasite.

Finally, Grace, you must be firm. Mistaken affection easily blinds us to the true good of those we love. We see this every day in parent-child relationships. Because you have such a long habit of sacrificing yourself for your family, you may be inclined to give in all too easily. Remember, what you really want is your sister's greatest good. Think of what she will be like in ten or fifteen years if you are not firm in helping her now. It's generally easy to exploit charity, but those who try it are not really benefited, and we're not truly charitable in allowing them to get away with it.

Why Doesn't the Church
Drop Some of Its Outmoded
Customs About Marriage?

Why does the Church create such a stir about getting married? You'd almost think she was against it. When Myrtle and I went to her pastor about our marriage, he insisted that the banns had to be read in both our churches though we've lived there most of our lives. To top it off, he wants us to come in for instructions. As if anybody old enough to marry in our day and age didn't know what he was getting into? Why doesn't the Church drop some of these outmoded customs?

∾∾∾∾∾∾

I SUPPOSE a good number of young people feel as you do about many Church laws governing marriage, Jack. Of course, the obvious answer is that the Church has been in the marriage business for about twenty centuries and probably knows the ins and outs of the trade pretty well by now. Experience can be a good teacher, particularly if people are willing to learn. And Churchmen have been willing to learn because they are deeply interested in saving souls and in protecting the dignity of a sacrament.

The rules of which you speak, Jack, are not mere residues or carry-overs from the distant past. The Code of canon law which embodies these rules is revised according to changing conditions and times. The last big revision of the Code was published in 1918, and frequent minor changes have been added since then, so its laws can hardly be considered outmoded.

Now, let's take another look at your problems. You feel the publication of banns in your case is not necessary. As you probably have been told, the Code states that on three successive Sundays or feast days of obligation before marriage is to be celebrated, the names of those who are about to contract marriage must be announced at the principal mass, and the faithful are informed that they are gravely obliged to make known to the proper authorities any impediments or reasons why this couple should not marry. Only the bishop can dispense from the publications of the banns.

Why does the Church insist on the banns? Obviously, to protect the marriage contract. Experience shows that some people have concealed a previous marriage or some other impediment and attempted marriage even though they were not free to do so. This type is still around, as any experienced pastor will tell you, so the Church tries to protect its innocent members from them by this rule.

Second, you are surprised that the pastor insists on giving you instructions. You feel that Myrtle and you know what marriage is about or you wouldn't enter it. You're probably right, Jack, but there are several other points to consider here. The pastor uses these instruction periods as an additional means of finding out if impediments to a valid contract exist and also to assure himself that both of you are entering marriage with full knowledge and consent. He cannot in conscience officiate at the ceremony unless he does this.

Furthermore, Jack, I think you must recognize that marriage involves many new situations having serious moral implications. Both of you must clearly understand the rights and obligations you are about to acquire.

Finally, marriage is a sacrament, and your pastor will want to make sure that you know what this means. As a way of life leading to perfection, it includes both aids and obstacles to mutual sanctification. It is well to review these now, lest you miss the full flowering of your life together.

Considering the Church's position from another viewpoint, we can see that the banns and instructions serve an additional purpose. Because of the delay they necessarily involve, they help prevent those thoughtless, hurried marriages all too common today. Studies have shown that the requirement of even a relatively brief delay cuts down the number of civil marriages considerably. We have no reason to doubt that the same factors are operative among Catholics.

You may be interested, Jack, in hearing of an experience I had concerning the Church's rules on this point. I was asked to lecture on the Catholic viewpoint before a graduate sociology class in one of our large secular universities. As I discovered from the comments afterwards, all these young sociologists were greatly impressed by the wisdom of the Church in requiring banns and instructions. They all felt that Catholic couples were getting a real break here and wondered whether the practice couldn't be generalized.

I believe if you give it a little further thought, Jack, both you and Myrtle will recognize that the Church is doing what it can to help make your marriage and that of other couples a real success.

To Spank or Not
to Spank . . .
That's the Question

*Putting it bluntly, should children be spanked when they
have proved themselves naughty enough to deserve the
"old fashioned treatment"? Until approximately what age
should parents feel it their duty to "paddle Mary or
Johnny from the rear"? Our friends tell us our children
—ages 10, 12, and 14—are too old to be spanked. We
don't agree with them. Our spankings are mild—a few
little hand taps while turned over our knee. Are we
wrong?*

❧❧❧❧❧❧

A S YOU probably know, Alice, ideas about how to raise
children shift from one extreme to another every few
years. In the late twenties, the psychologist Watson told
parents to treat children like adults. "If you must, kiss them
once on the forehead when they say goodnight. Shake hands
with them in the morning." Contemporary parents took him
literally, though the next generation shifted to the opposite
extreme of utter permissiveness. Today parents turn to the
more balanced writing of Spock and Gesell to learn about
their growing children.

In spite of numerous theories and some research, we still
have little scientifically verified knowledge about the long

range effects of early training experience upon children. Hence prudence prompts us to offer no general theory of the merits or demerits of spanking, rather we shall raise a few questions and suggest a few norms.

What is the purpose of spanking? Obviously it is not an outlet for the anger or exasperation of the parent. Children are spanked with the hope of improving their behavior—as we commonly say, to teach them a lesson.

It follows, first, that some children may never need a spanking. They have a naturally docile, happy disposition which requires little more than a look or a word for discipline. The majority, however, have their moments of rebellion, self-ishness, or meanness to others when they can't be reasoned with and need to be disciplined. Likewise, in situations involving serious danger for the child or others, disobedience must be associated with physical pain, since reasoning with him has failed. It's silly to let a child learn from experience when that experience may seriously harm him or others.

Second, since spankings are meant to help the child, they should be used intelligently. This is to say, a child should clearly understand why he is being punished. He obviously should not be punished for an accident, or for something he could not reasonably be expected to foresee. Punishment should be consistent. If you spank him for being "sassy" spank him every time it happens. Don't carelessly threaten him with punishment, and then spank him only when you're exasperated. Further, if you feel he deserves a spanking, give him his due and then let him remain by himself for awhile so he can think it over. Don't spoil the lesson by getting sentimental about it.

Until what age should children be spanked? I feel that depends very much upon the child. In reality, spankings are necessary because at some stages of their development, children cannot be reasoned with and their disobedience must be associated with pain or some discomfort they can grasp. As they develop, reason and self-discipline gradually become operative, and other means of securing conformity to rules become available.

Of course, the final objective of the whole training process is to enable children to master the norms, rules, and controls required for mature Christian living. Some mature more quickly than others, but the goal is the same for all. Perhaps the method is not as important as the correct objective: to teach children to stand on their own feet, and make their own decisions in terms of correct Christian principles. This requires the habit of reflection, self-control, and responsibility.

Should you continue to spank, Alice? I rather think there are other means of achieving the same objective with your children at their age. Of course, the main point is that you keep clearly in mind what you are trying to do as parents, that is, to help your children develop toward the independence and responsibility of Christian maturity.

Rights in Marriage
Impose a Corresponding
Obligation

Many of us older family folks have a serious problem—
when and how to call a halt in increasing our family.
At 37, I'm married 15 years, and carry my seventh child.
My strength and my husband's income would do nicely
with four or five—as it is, I'm constantly running out of
both. My husband considers his impulses as God-given
and to be fully exercised—God will provide! Can you
give us some guidance?

≈≈≈≈≈≈≈

"OLDER family folks," as you call them, Martha, are
not the only ones who seem confused about the
rights and duties of married life. Questions related to this
problem arise so frequently that the most helpful approach
will probably be to spell out a few pertinent principles and
facts applicable to all of them. Some of these may appear to
be self-evident and repetitious, but experience has taught me
they are not.

First, husbands and wives differ considerably in the
nature of their reproductive drive, the personal implications
of its fruitful use for their future, and consequently in their
attitudes toward the exercise of this faculty in marriage. Likewise, wide individual differences exist; while age, health,

293

family responsibilities, and so forth, cause further variations. Hence, chances are that few couples will always reach perfect agreement in this area. This does not mean that there need be conflict. Most couples soon discover that though they may not agree on a great number of things, they can learn to adjust and adapt if they wish to succeed.

Second, the use of the reproductive faculty is a human act, an act of the person, not the mere unrestricted exercise of a bodily function. Hence it implies the acceptance of full responsibility for its possible consequences by the couple as a couple. Some husbands are selfishly irresponsible in this regard, forgetting that they must seriously consider the health and strength of their wives, and also their own ability to make reasonable provision for another child. Marriage would cease to be human if the rights it conferred carried no corresponding obligations, and consequently no need for self-control.

Third, because we are not controlled by instinct but possess the use of reason, we are constantly "putting asunder what God has joined together." The Creator meant conjugal relations to be a mysterious, unifying act of love which He would bless with new life under proper conditions and which would strengthen and support the marriage bond throughout life. But husbands and wives frequently put asunder this marvelous unity of shared, mutual pleasure and love either by ignoring its dignity or emphasizing its merely physical aspects. As a result, it loses its true significance and is used for selfish purposes.

Fourth, the marriage contract confers equal conjugal rights upon husband and wife, but the use of these rights is subordinated to the primary purpose of marriage, which is the procreation and education of children. Briefly, these rights may not be used selfishly but for the good of the couple and of the family. This requires self-control and a Christian sense of responsibility.

Turning now to your "older folks" problem, Martha, your letter makes clear that your husband has put his own interpretation on Catholic teaching about marriage. Of course you must trust in God, but this trust should not be a thinly disguised excuse for selfish indulgence and lack of Christian restraint. I know he will protest that restraint is difficult under the circumstances—has he ever tried it? Has he made use of prayer and the sacraments to gain strength? Has he shared the burdens of rearing a large family by helping with the children around the home? Unless he can answer all these questions in the affirmative, he had best examine his conscience very seriously.

What can you do? Well, if he will cooperate, you should practice continence either periodic or absolute after your baby arrives, until you have regained your health, and your financial situation is under control. Of course, this may not be easy but many Christian couples have shown that it is possible with a little mutual cooperation and the help of grace.

Somewhere in the past, marital chastity acquired a merely negative meaning in people's mind—the avoidance of contraceptives. But chastity in all walks of life is something positive: the control and regulation of our reproductive faculties according to the rule of right reason. Your husband has evidently forgotten this.

How to
Keep Busy
at Forty

What about the healthy, capable, forty-year-old wife and mother whose children are in school and are demanding less of her attention? Not interested in consuming time via bridge and gossip. Attractive home and yard and entertaining can be managed readily and still time and energy to use. I'm sure you will come up with some interesting insights, and many of us women need direction.

∾∾∾∾∾∾

YOU'VE really put me on the spot this time, Jane! I must confess that the drive and endurance of many of you modern mothers is a source of constant wonder to me. You perform such a variety of tasks quickly, efficiently, and with energy to spare that the old term "weaker sex" obviously no longer applies. Perhaps it never did.

Of course, changes in our traditional family system have operated in favor of women. Because families have declined so sharply in size, the usual span of the childbearing years has become only about half as long as it was two generations ago. The average mother whose family reached completion in 1890 had borne 5.4 children, with an estimated interval of ten years between marriage and the birth of the last child. She had not given birth to her last child until she was about

32 years old. Mothers who reached the end of their reproductive period in 1952 averaged only 2.35 children, and
roughly fifty per cent had borne their last child by the time
they were 26 years old. The present "baby boom" may modify
this trend somewhat, though there is evidence to suggest that
early age at marriage and the tendency to confine childbearing
to the period while the wife is still young may not greatly
extend the age at which she bears her last child.

These changes, together with many improvements in
home making and housekeeping, have left many forty-year-old
mothers with considerable freedom and leisure. You tell me,
Jane, that they are looking for direction. I think it would be
foolhardy for me to attempt to spell out explicit directives.
Indeed, I fancy a good many mothers already regard me with
a jaundiced eye because I've used the words *freedom* and
leisure! These are relative terms. If and to the extent that
they apply, I would venture the following suggestions.

First, I'm happy to see that you have avoided typical
escapes and timekillers like gossip, bridge, and so forth.

Second, I'm glad that you don't feel a compulsion to
spend all of your time in housekeeping. Some women fall
into a rut in this regard and keep cleaning, dusting, and pol-
ishing away whether it is needed or not.

Third, you might check your participation in school,
church, and community affairs. When your family required
most of your time, your cooperation in these was necessarily
restricted. There may be real need for you now that you
have more time.

Fourth, the needs of your children will vary as they continue to grow. Spend some time helping them plan their
recreation, studies, and future vocation.

Fifth, this is an excellent time to seek closer companionship with your husband. The early childbearing and child-rearing stages often keep mother and father so busy at separate tasks that they lose some of the close unity they enjoyed when they started marriage. As you gradually start to "launch" your children and face the "empty nest," it is well to prepare for the long years ahead you will enjoy as a couple. This is a new stage in your family cycle and requires some adjustment.

Sixth, it would be a mistake to concentrate only on external activities. At forty, you are approaching the end of your distinctive feminine function of reproduction, but as a person you face some thirty more years of life. Now is the time for new intellectual and spiritual growth. Up to the present, your interests were necessarily confined to the home and the performance of countless routines. Now you must enlarge your interests, renew your intellectual life, and deepen your knowledge and practice of religion. This isn't "highbrow" stuff, Jane. As your children develop, you must grow yourself both to aid them and to retain real contact with them. You and your husband both may need to enlarge your intellectual horizons, and in this, you may well be the leader. There is much to read and discuss. Perhaps there are other couples in your neighborhood who have the same needs. Although study clubs and discussion groups are not essential, they can serve a useful purpose.

Finally, all that I have said, Jane, can be summarized by saying, don't get bogged down by retreating from life or in meaningless escapes. Renew, enlarge, and deepen your spiritual and intellectual interests in whatever way appeals to you. This should keep you busy for the next thirty years.

At Confirmation, He Took a Pledge not to Drink Until 21

What do you think about drinking in mixed company or on dates? At almost every party we teenagers attend, liquor is served and taken by nearly all of us. When I asked one boy why he didn't drink, he said that he had taken a pledge at confirmation not to drink any alcoholic beverages until he was twenty-one. That got me! I guess all of us took the same pledge, yet we sometimes drink at home with our parents as well as at parties. Aren't we doing wrong?

≈≈≈≈≈≈≈

YOU have two problems, Michael, and I'd best answer them separately. First, what about drinking in mixed company or on dates? I think we can answer that one rather easily if we analyze the effects of alcohol on the user. We should consider these from two points of view: what science tells us it does physiologically, and what people think it does or feel it does psychologically. As we shall see, the two are closely related, though they appear as contradictions.

Considered in its physiological effects, alcohol is not a stimulant but a depressant or narcotic, affecting the higher brain centers first and dulling their action. Since these centers are related to reason, judgment, and conscience, when they are affected by alcohol, these human powers are depressed and become less active.

Considered psychologically, alcohol, at least in small amounts, appears to be a stimulant. A drink is said to give one a "lift," and tired people take a drink or two for a "pick-up." You probably have noticed that parties become noisier and livelier once everybody has had a drink or two.

If alcohol is really a depressant, why does it apparently stimulate us? Well, Michael, when alcohol is taken in moderate quantities, it seems this effect is partly the result of our imagination—we feel we ought to feel stimulated; and partly the result of its depressant effects on the judgment centers of our brain—we relax our habitual controls and inhibitions.

With these facts in mind, let's consider drinking on dates. In the first place, why should young people feel so worn out and tired that they require such a lift? Further, although alcohol is not a sexual stimulant, it does depress the judgment centers of the brain, thus lowering self-control and consequently offering free play to the normally strong tendency in youth to seek sexual stimulation under the guise of displaying affection.

Young people who drink on dates are clearly asking for trouble. Unfortunately, all too many recognize this only after it is too late. This applies to college as well as high school students, though the tendency of youth to pose as grown-ups by aping their elders is so strong that many will continue to ignore the facts of common experience.

Your second problem, Michael, is not so easily answered. I'm not sure what explanation of the abstinence pledge is given at confirmation, or how well it is understood by young people and their parents. It would seem that it must either be inadequately explained or else considered some type of conditional promise; otherwise it would be difficult to account for the widespread violations you report. One thing is certain, a group pledge taken under such circumstances does not bind under sin. To my knowledge, the pledge is not given in all parishes, so you had best ask your own pastor how he interprets it.

As your letter suggests, this whole problem of youthful drinking is treated rather lightly by most people. Although there should be no objection if young people drink at home with their parents according to various family customs, there can be no need or justification for drinking on dates and in mixed company. Some young people drink because they are afraid to differ from the crowd; some because they feel bashful and insecure; and others because they wish to appear sophisticated and grown up.

None of these reasons carry much weight with normal boys or girls, who have learned to stand on their own feet by this time and feel no need to impress others by aping older people. Young people who feel they must drink on dates or at parties in order to enjoy themselves are openly confessing that they are incapable of sharing in social life without some stimulant. I think you'll agree, Michael, this is a sign of weakness, either emotional or physical. Wouldn't vitamins be more in order, or is it just their imagination?

Girls in Senior High School
Want to Wear
Engagement Rings

Why can't senior girls in Catholic high schools wear engagement rings on their fingers? I'm told that over half the seniors are engaged and wear their rings pinned inside their uniforms with the pin showing so everyone knows they are engaged. This is a big event for girls. They display the rings outside of school and, besides everyone knows they're engaged. What is gained by making them resentful of school discipline?

❦❦❦❦❦❦❦

WELL, Janie, a good many teachers and students have discussed this question at length during the past few years. I gather from your letter that the decision has gone against the students in your city and possibly in others. It may help clarify our thinking if we review some of the pertinent aspects of the problem.

As you are probably aware, the age at which people enter marriage has dropped considerably since 1940. White couples tend to marry somewhat younger than nonwhite. During the past few years close to one-half of the first-married brides married before reaching their twentieth birthday. Indeed, about one-third of all first-married brides married at ages 18 and 19.

These are national statistics, and we have no way of knowing how fully they apply to the Catholic segment of the population, though there is little reason to believe that Catholics differ from the general population in this regard. It follows that a good number of senior girls in high school may be engaged. Whether this is true of over half, as you report, I'm not prepared to say, but I really doubt it is so in most high schools.

What is the purpose of an engagement ring? Obviously it is a sign or symbol that a certain young couple have agreed to marry and wish the public to know about it. Girls are usually very proud of their rings, so that it is easy to understand their resentment at not being allowed to wear them while at school.

What is the purpose of the prohibition? Clearly it is not against either the idea of engagement rings or of marriage. However, many teachers feel that this concern with rings, marriages, and so forth, has no place within the school. It is bound to be a source of distraction to the other girls, particularly those in the lower classes. At the same time, many teachers feel that girls are generally too young and inexperienced to marry as soon as they finish high school. By forbidding them to wear their engagement rings around school, they believe they may decrease distractions from this source and possibly discourage some girls from entering such immature marriages.

I feel these are the pertinent facts and assumptions in the case. What do I think about this prohibition? Frankly, Janie, I believe that it doesn't accomplish its purpose, creates unnecessary resentment, probably weakens the lasting influence of teachers on their students, and consequently had best be discontinued. Granting that such early marriages might well be discouraged in most cases, I don't think this is either an effective or reasonable way to accomplish it.

Such early engagements occur because boys and girls have been keeping company for some time. This is clearly a parental problem and should be handled by them. Under these circumstances, the school will best fulfill its function if students are offered adequate instruction concerning the Catholic viewpoint on dating, courtship, and marriage. As a remedy for early engagements, this instruction would obviously come too late if provided only in the senior year, though it were better given here than not at all. Since roughly four out of five girls don't go on to college, whatever formal marriage courses they are to receive must be given in high school.

Your question touches upon a relatively small problem, Janie, but back of it looms the distressing dilemma of adolescent boy-girl relationships in our society. The toleration, if not promotion, of early dating, steady dating, and unsupervised association between boys and girls years before they are mature enough to reasonably contemplate marriage should cause parents and teachers alike to question some of their attitudes and practices. What are they doing to meet the overall problem?

By the way, Janie, are you a senior with a concealed engagement ring?

One Day, My Wife
Won't Stop Talking;
the Next, She Won't Talk

We've been married six months now, and I still can't figure my wife out. Like the other evening, I knew she'd been crying about something, but do you think she'd tell me? Some days when I'm tired, she wears me out with talking; at other times, she clams up and shows no interest in what I want to tell her. These are only a few examples. Do you think we're incompatible?

∿∿∿∿∿∿∿

YOU probably are, Frank, for as Chesterton once remarked, "Men and women are incompatible by nature." It would be little short of a miracle if you and your wife always felt the same way, were emotionally up or down on the same days, and felt like talking or being silent at the same times. Unfortunately, there's been so much talk about the need for "compatibility" in building a successful marriage that many young couples feel they're just not meant for each other if they don't find perfect agreement.

In going over much of the modern literature on the subject, I get the impression that only two colorless morons would meet all the specifications required for perfect compatibility. In reality, this thinking is based on a defective psychology which assumes that people have a basic personality structure that can't be modified or adapted. Hence if husband and wife discover that they have dissimilar personalities, they're caught in a hopeless situation and may as well head for the divorce court at once.

What does Chesterton's remark really mean, Frank? Obviously, that men and women, as two distinct expressions of human nature, are necessarily different; and with the French, most of us would agree: *"vive la difference!"* But there's more to it than that. No two women—or two men—are quite alike.

Since marriage involves such constant, intimate companionship, it brings out the individual masculine and feminine differences of husband and wife in full contrast. Dating and courtship do this to some extent, but they are relatively shallow associations in comparison with marriage. Whether they recognize it or not, most couples put on their best behavior during courtship. In the routine intimacy of marriage, they appear as they really are.

Hence only in marriage do couples start getting acquainted with each other to any marked degree. The process takes time, starting in earnest as soon as the novelty and emotional effervescence of first intimacy wears off. In this sense, we can say that marriage really begins only after the honeymoon has failed.

This does not mean that marriage is a dull, monotonous routine into which you have been tricked by your emotions. It can become such only for shallow couples who make no attempt to understand and appreciate each other's diverse qualities. Some fail to do this because they foolishly believe that they know each other perfectly already; while others are so immature and self-centered that they simply ignore the richness and distinctiveness of their partner's character.

How can you go about getting better acquainted with

your wife? Paradoxically, Frank, the first step is to become better acquainted with yourself. You need greater insight into your own character, your changing moods, interests, and dispositions. Reflect on your own need for encouragement, friendship, attention, and affection. Analyze your motives, your reactions to success or failure, your own emotional ups and downs.

Second, once you have gained some insight into yourself, apply this knowledge to your wife. Try to put yourself in her position. She too is an individual, with her distinctive moods, reactions, and personal needs. These are different from your own, of course, but they make her what she is, the woman you loved and married. Like yourself, she also seeks happiness and fulfillment in marriage.

Third, if adjustments must be made, remember, Frank, you must both make them. In marriage you are helpmates, partners, supporting one another, and helping to carry each other's burdens. You can do this from day to day only to the extent that you understand each other.

You want your marriage to be a steady growth in companionship and love, but love depends upon knowledge. As your married life unfolds, you will have many opportunities to see how little you really understand yourself—and your wife. You will profit from these only if you are now aware of your ignorance. Remember, you and your wife represent two distinct human images of God. Know and respect these differences and they will become sources of love, not incompatibility.

What's Wrong with
Marriage Preparation
Courses in College

I'm really worried about the advice our young Catholic students are receiving in their marriage classes. They are told to move as far as possible from all parents—to put up barriers whenever possible! That parents have one objective in mind and that is to cling to the child, and that all parents interfere to a certain extent. What do you think of such advice?

※※※※※※

WELL, May, if I told you, they couldn't print it, so I had best skip my comments on such nonsense. I sincerely hope that this advice is not handed out as generally as you infer, though I must admit that the evidence you present from several different colleges looks rather disconcerting.

It is possible that some marriage preparation courses leave this impression because of the emphasis they place on in-law problems. Since such problems may occur, they should be discussed, but it would be quite illogical to try to eliminate them by doing away with in-laws. Problems also may occur in choosing friends, the use of money, and in conjugal relations, yet no counselor would advise young couples to move as far away from these areas as possible in order to avoid the threat of conflict. Such hasty generalizations throw the baby out with the bath water. Granting that some in-laws may become the source of trouble, it is patently absurd to conclude that in-laws as such are dangerous. As the French say, "One swallow in the sky doesn't make spring."

On the other hand, May, it would be unrealistic to deny that the formation of smooth relationships between parents and married children calls for considerable mutual adjustment. Marriage will take your children out of your immediate family circle and place them in another of their own making. This will necessarily modify your relationships to them and vice versa. Henceforth, their primary loyalties must focus on their own conjugal unit, while on the basis of their new unity as a couple, they must pattern their relationships to two sets of parents. Studies suggest that this process takes time, though it is normally accomplished without serious conflict. Both parents and children must recognize and accept the implications of marriage. Both may promote or hinder smooth adjustment. In-law relationships are a two way street!

The adjustment I'm talking about should not be viewed as a problem but as a normal process. Marriage unites two established families and starts a third. This is precisely its strength—the new conjugal unit benefits from the support, encouragement, and affection of the older units, while parents rejoice in the extension of their family to include new members and new generations. Indeed, I have constantly insisted that one of the major sources of weakness in our present family system is the lack of support young couples receive from their circle of relatives. This often results from high rates of mobility and rapid social change. To set it up as an ideal appears unintelligible to me.

You have reason to worry if your children receive such

advice. Tell them to use their common sense and forget it. It will be much more profitable to consider what is needed for adjustment. Hence I would suggest that some thought be given to the following. First, both sets of parents must be given equal consideration and affection.

Second, it is normal for girls to retain rather close emotional attachment to their mothers. After all, they've known each other for quite some time. Some young husbands resent this, as if they had a rival. Third, prudent parents will not try to help their young couples too much, at least in the beginning. Let them make their own plans and face their own normal problems.

Fourth, parents will wisely refrain from taking sides in strictly marital disagreements. Let the young people work it out on their own terms. It's their problem and can be really settled only by themselves. If it proves too much for them, both sets of parents should cooperate in helping them work out a solution. This may sound idealistic, but remember, when the success of sacramental marriage is at stake, parents must move humbly and cautiously lest they dare put asunder what God has joined together.

Finally, particularly in the beginning, relationships between parents and married children should be affectionate but flexible. This is to say, don't start out by setting aside definite days each week or month for family reunions. Such schedules frequently become restricting and consequently distasteful to one or both parties.

Domineering Mothers
Are a Type,
but Not All Alike

I'm twenty-one and presently "disengaged" again. It's George's mother. She wants to run our lives as she does everything else. The present clash resulted from her insistence on buying us a house near her. When I refused and George sided with me, she faked a heart attack, so George gave in. Back went his ring! George is not a weakling but he's no match for her tricks. Is there any hope that we can work this out?

※※※※※

THE answer, Mary, is probably *yes*, framed in a border of "ifs." But before discussing your problem, I wish to compliment you on refusing to drift into marriage with the romantic hope that all problems will be settled once you've made your trip to the altar. Whatever may be the merits of your stand, you were wise in postponing your marriage until the relationship with your future in-laws was thoroughly clarified. The time to settle such problems is before marriage —only then can you still give back his ring.

Now, Mary, let's look at your problem. First, strong, efficient mothers who are accustomed to dominating their family circle are not all alike. A good many of them have assumed this role either because they are very capable or because they had to under the circumstances. They became very efficient at running the family; but unfortunately, like many efficiency experts, they sometimes tend to forget the human elements involved. Often with the best intentions in the world, they dominate the lives of their maturing children, even to the extent of trying to control their marriages. Since they are not used to meeting opposition in their own family circle, they regard the independence of an "outsider" as a nuisance and may consequently resent it.

At this point, another type of dominating mother may emerge. Although the majority sooner or later resign themselves to the fact that their children have grown up, a few refuse to accept it and use every possible "trick," as you put it, to maintain control. George's mother seems to fall in this type.

Second, the real question you must answer, however, does not concern your future mother-in-law, but George. When children have been raised in a mother-dominated home, two general types may result. One may be quite normal, though perhaps somewhat immature in decision-making and self-assertion. The second may be a product of what the psychiatrists call "momism." Their dependence is so deeply interwoven into their personality from childhood that they are lost without "mom." Actually, they are incapable of mature family relationships, and one who marries them soon discovers that he has acquired a child, not a partner.

So you see, Mary, you'll have to make sure that George isn't this latter type. You describe him as "no weakling," and since his mother had to take drastic measures to scare him, I rather think he's normal but a little slow in asserting himself.

What should you do? First, you'd better have a good,

calm, objective talk with George, in which you explain that although you respect his love for his mother, he must choose between her and you when it comes to planning the future. He'll probably agree, but protest he doesn't want to hurt her either. Your next step is to formulate a plan of action. You may discover that she controls George's finances. Get this changed at once. Next, go ahead and make definite plans about your marriage. If you can marry within the near future, pick out an apartment or home, see your pastor about a possible date, and when things are pretty well lined up, tell your parents what preparations you have made. Then wait for the explosion. If his mother sees the game is up, she may concede the victory—for the time being. If she puts on an act, both of you should now know how to interpret it.

Finally, in forming your plans for the future, it will be best to steer clear of all your immediate in-laws for the first year or two until you have become firmly established in your own marriage. This sounds rather drastic, and it is, but the situation calls for it. You have to learn to work together as partners, and to develop deep loyalty through shared experiences before you can run the risk of possible outside interference.

Does this program sound too difficult, Mary? Well, it has been carried out successfully by others. One final word, make no concessions. If George doesn't want to follow through, he's free to choose, but then drop him at once and absolutely. It would be a serious mistake to drag such an affair on further. Give George back to "mom," and find yourself a man.

Our Boy and His Girl
Threaten to Marry
Without Our Consent

Do the parents of an eighteen-year-old boy have the right to withhold their consent to his marriage in an effort to try and prevent his marrying at this time? Our boy will soon be nineteen and has two more years to go serving in the Marine Corps. His girl is about the same age. They have stumped our every argument and now threaten to marry without our consent. Her parents finally gave their consent, but I don't feel right about it. What can I do?

❧❧❧❧❧❧

I THINK you've answered your first question yourself, Amy. You have the right, but what good will it do to refuse consent if they intend to get married anyway? Under the circumstances, I think the most prudent approach is to grant your consent provided they show they have given serious thought to the following problems.

Where are they going to set up housekeeping? Is she going to live with her folks during the next two years? Move about from place to place with him, living either on the base or off of it as the conditions may require? If he is sent out of the country for a time, will she follow him or remain here?

Will the presence of a baby affect their plans concerning living arrangements? They are a young couple. It is highly likely that the bride will become pregnant within the next two years provided they do not employ immoral contraceptive measures. Are they realistically facing the consequences of possible future pregnancies in terms of travel, expense, housing, separation, and so forth? Many couples in such circumstances enter marriage with the intention that the bride will be employed while the husband is in the service. This doesn't indicate very realistic thinking on the part of young couples who are bound to observe the moral law pertaining to marital relations.

Have they considered the problems involved in securing early marriage adjustment under the changing, unsettled, conditions of military service? All marriages start out as relatively fragile, shallow associations, no matter how great the emotional display may appear. Through shared experience, deeper understanding, and mutual adaptation the couple gradually grow together and establish the firm bonds of an unbreakable union. When the husband is in military service, it is extremely difficult to provide the conditions which foster the growth of such unity.

In my analysis of hundreds of broken war marriages, I discovered that the source of the difficulty was pretty much the same in all. The newlyweds were unable to establish durable marriage relationships under the circumstances. Shared experiences were too few. The common feelings, attitudes, and ideals essential to enduring unity had not been given time to form. Particularly among young couples who were forced to live apart for a time, it was discovered that they knew too little of each other to foster growth in mutual understanding and sympathy through the medium of letters. Frequently, their reunion proved disillusioning for one or both partners because they discovered that they had grown apart rather than together and now as husband and wife had very little in common.

Have they thought about what they will do after the two-year stretch is finished? Adjustment to civilian life and employment after leaving military service is difficult enough for most boys; it may prove extremely trying for a young husband who must provide for a wife and possible family.

I think you should put these questions to the young couple honestly and without emotion. Marriage is a life vocation based on a holy, sacramental contract. In all fairness to themselves, they should enter it under conditions best calculated to make it a success.

Finally, why are they in such a hurry to get married? Obviously, to enjoy marital partnership and companionship. More basic, though frequently unrecognized in such cases, is the difficulty of observing premarital chastity under the circumstances. In this connection, Amy, you should point out to them that the observance of marital chastity also demands a great deal of restraint and self-control from Christian spouses. Many young couples fail to recognize this and hurry into marriage as an answer to all their problems.

With these facts before them, why don't you suggest that the girl get a job and that they both start saving and planning for a future marriage which can be started with much greater hope of happiness and success? Two years added to their young lives will put them at just about the right age for marriage.

Diet Fad Has Hit My Wife;
She's Impossible
to Live With

How can I get my wife to stop dieting? When she goes on one of her hunger strikes, it's almost impossible to live with her. Naturally she's grouchy and short-tempered when she's half starved, but I don't think it's right that the children and I should have to suffer while she's fighting her battle of the bulge. She's not really overweight anyway, she just wants to look younger than she is. How can I handle this problem?

≈≈≈≈≈

JACK, I'm afraid you're asking me to walk in where angels fear to tread! Most women have their own ideas about dieting, and, right or wrong, I don't think we can do much to change them. Not that their decision to diet is wholly arbitrary, but their reasons for it range from following a current fad to sheer necessity.

In all honesty, we must admit that many American women have their problems in this regard. Because of our cult of youth, the feminine ideal is depicted not as a motherly matron but an immature woman. The lithe, emaciated creatures who typically serve as models have figures which tend to be more masculine than feminine. Our much publicized "beauty queens" are girls rather than women. This emphasis on masculinity and youth is something of a paradox in a society in which the average woman is a mother and lives to be seventy.

Further, many American wives are made overly conscious of their weight by the dire predictions of "beauty" experts, advertisers, and magazine writers that they may lose their husbands if they don't retain their girlish figures. Evidently, American husbands remain incurably youthful.

Finally, the modern family cycle works somewhat to the disadvantage of women in this regard. During the early stages of the cycle, they are too busy bearing and raising children to think of anything else. Once the last child is off to school, the pressure slackens a bit, wives have more time to take stock of themselves, and they may become suddenly aware that they are no longer girls but mature women. Some may dislike the physical implications of this change and fight desperately to remain youthful. Others may discover that the past busy years made them somewhat careless about their appearance, and they wisely decide to correct the situation.

So you see, Jack, the problem of dieting has many different aspects. Wives protest that they are blamed if they let themselves go, and mocked if they try to reduce. Modern society offers them no appropriate models at this stage. They feel too young to accept the usual advice to "grow old gracefully," yet if they try to remain girls, nature is against them, and they have to fight every step of the way.

What's the best way to handle your problem? First, it will help to try to see things from your wife's viewpoint. Why is she worried about her weight? Maybe she thinks she's been too careless in the past. Perhaps she feels a little insecure. Some women do at this time of life. Have you been taking her pretty much for granted? Do you notice it when she wears something new? When was the last time you told her how nice she looked in a certain outfit? Or do you think she's too old to appreciate compliments?

Second, you can sympathize with what she's trying to do. You may not want her to diet, Jack, but you can show her that you understand her problem and are willing to cooperate. Dieting makes some people short-tempered, first, because they resent having to use this means, and second, because they have to do it alone. A little sympathy will go a long way here, even if dieting is solely her own idea.

Finally, why not cooperate with her by suggesting some alternatives? Some couples drive out into the country or go to the park and take a hike together. It will be good for both of you. There are well-designed exercises for keeping in trim; suggest some of these, since most people tend to use only certain sets of muscles in their daily work. Provide opportunities for your wife to get out socially; encourage her to become interested in some outside activities if she can spare the time.

Let's be honest, Jack, none of the above methods will make her lose a pound, but they will help both her figure and her disposition. Remember, you're partners. She has a problem; either you help solve it satisfactorily, or you must take the consequences. In marriage, either you solve your problems together, or you suffer separately.

Godparents Take
Duties of Sponsorship
Seriously

I'm terribly worried about the religious training of one of my godchildren. She's my brother's child, aged seven, and the oldest of three. My brother is very careless about religion. His wife is non-Catholic, an excellent mother but indifferent toward all faiths. When we visit them, they are evasive about the religious training of the children. They know their obligations in this regard, but I'm afraid they do nothing. What can I do?

※※※※※

YOU are to be commended, Mary, for taking the duties of sponsorship seriously. Some sponsors forget that they have a serious obligation to look after the Christian education and spiritual training of their spiritual children. Of course, the care of children falls principally upon parents. When they neglect their duties, however, sponsors must do what they can to assure the religious instruction and formation of their godchildren.

This is the situation which confronts you now, Mary. It is clearly not an easy one to handle. Your obligations both as sponsor and near relative are clear. The question is, what can you, a mere "outsider" do to fulfill them? Your problem is further complicated by the fact that you do not live very near your brother's family so that it is difficult to learn what religious training the children receive.

Under the circumstances, I would suggest the following approach. First, your brother should be reminded of his serious obligation to offer a good example to his children, and to guarantee their Christian education. I gather from your letter that you have attempted to do this without much success. However, as their children start growing up, most parents feel the need of giving them some moral guidance and training. Try to impress upon your brother that if he really loves his children, he will not let them face the temptations and trials of adolescence without the guidance and motivation which comes from religion. It is a matter of common experience that even lukewarm or careless parents frequently come to their senses when they think of the needs of their growing children, so keep after your brother prudently in this regard.

Second, I think you should be very careful in dealing with your sister-in-law concerning the training of her children. As you say, she is an excellent mother, but since she does not personally appreciate the need for religion, she may well resent any outside advice or interference. She knows her obligations, yet because of her own views, she isn't going to do much about carrying them out as you feel she should. In this situation, perhaps the best you can do is to avoid antagonizing her, lest in self-defense she takes a definite stand against religion and communicates this attitude to her children.

Third, while the children are growing up, it is important that they come to know you and your family as models of Christian kindness and charity. Your example in living the faith will have more lasting effects upon them than anything you may say. If they learn to love and admire you, they will find it natural to want to imitate your way of life, particularly when they are old enough to think for themselves. Above all, be careful how you speak about religion to them while they are still young. Whatever you do in this regard must not be taken as a criticism of their home training. Their first loyalty is naturally to their parents, and they will only be confused or resentful of criticism leveled against those they love.

Finally, Mary, together with giving a good example, your most important obligation is prayer. Commend them humbly to Christ and His Blessed Mother. Keep their needs constantly in mind when you pray. This is a long range approach. Year after year throughout life, keep them in your prayers. No matter how humanly hopeless the situation may appear at times, remember that we cannot see things from God's point of view. He accomplishes His purposes when and as He will. Our faith in prayer is based on His command, "Ask and you shall receive."

I suppose our greatest failure in fulfilling obligations of this kind is impatience. We want things done at once. We want them carried out according to our own plans. If our prayers are not answered at once, we think they are not being heard. This is a subtle form of pride, for it implies that we know what is best for ourselves and others. But only God sees the total picture. In His time, His own good time, He will answer our prayers.

Index

A NOTE ON THE TYPE

IN WHICH THIS BOOK IS SET

This book is set in Fairfield, a Linotype face, created by Rudolph Ruzicka, distinguished American artist and engraver. Introduced in 1940, Fairfield is almost strictly a book type with much charm and beauty. It is easy to read as one learns from extensive reading since it furnishes some degree of stimulation and pleasure to the eye. The fitting of each letter is practically perfect, which is a real tribute to its designer. This book was composed by Progressive Typographers, Inc., of York, Pa., printed by the Wickersham Printing Company of Lancaster, Pa. and bound by Moore and Company of Baltimore, Md. The typography and design by Howard N. King.